Feasting on the Word®

CHILDREN'S SERMONS
FOR YEAR A

Also available in this series

Feasting on the Word Children's Sermons for Year C

Feasting on the Word®

❧ CHILDREN'S SERMONS ❧
FOR YEAR A

Carol A. Wehrheim

WJK WESTMINSTER
JOHN KNOX PRESS
LOUISVILLE · KENTUCKY

© 2016 Carol A. Wehrheim

First edition
Published by Westminster John Knox Press
Louisville, Kentucky

16 17 18 19 20 21 22 23 24 25—10 9 8 7 6 5 4 3 2 1

Book design by Drew Stevens
Cover design by Lisa Buckley Design

Library of Congress Cataloging-in-Publication Data
Names: Wehrheim, Carol A., author.
Title: Feasting on the word : children's sermons for Year A / Carol A. Wehrheim.
Description: First edition. | Louisville, KY : Westminster John Knox Press, 2016. | Includes index.
Identifiers: LCCN 2016013574 (print) | LCCN 2016016934 (ebook) | ISBN 9780664261078 (pbk. : alk. paper) | ISBN 9781611646795 (ebk.)
Subjects: LCSH: Children's sermons. | Common lectionary (1992). Year A. | Church year sermons--Juvenile literature. | Preaching to children.
Classification: LCC BV4315 .W355 2016 (print) | LCC BV4315 (ebook) | DDC 252/.53—dc23
LC record available at https://lccn.loc.gov/2016013574

♾ The paper used in this publication meets the minimum requirements of the American National Standard for Information Sciences—Permanence of Paper for Printed Library Materials, ANSI Z39.48-1992.

Most Westminster John Knox Press books are available at special quantity discounts when purchased in bulk by corporations, organizations, and special-interest groups. For more information, please e-mail SpecialSales@wjkbooks.com.

*For all the children who have listened to my stories
and helped me polish my storytelling gifts*

Contents

LENT

EASTER

*During Ordinary Time, or the season after Pentecost, the lectionary offers two streams, or tracks, of readings: the semicontinuous and complementary streams of the Revised Common Lectionary. See page xviii of the introduction for more information.

Stories for Special Sundays

Acknowledgments

A number of years ago, I saw a notice of a storytelling workshop to be held on the Princeton University campus. It was a week-long seminar led by Susan Danoff. I didn't know Susan, but I wanted to know more about storytelling in the hope that I, a curriculum writer and editor, could find ways to write more engaging Bible stories for children. What I discovered in Susan was not only a spellbinding storyteller but also an excellent educator. I have described that week as the best week of continuing education I have experienced. From that seminar I learned not only how to tell a story; I also discovered the power of story. Since then, I have come to believe with more and more certainty that the church must regain its storytelling history, so that we tell the story to one another, face to face.

Many of the stories here are based on stories in the *Feasting on the Word* curriculum. Although I have written or revised them all, I have often been helped by a turn of phrase or point of view that was drawn from one of the writers for this series. I am especially indebted to Sharon Harding, who wrote many of the summer sessions and who gave me lovely words to begin as I wrote the Bible stories to tell to the congregation. Without the suggestion from David Maxwell that this book would be helpful to congregations, these stories would not be written down for others to tell.

There are few things I would rather do than tell Bible stories to children in church school or vacation Bible school or to the congregation in worship. I hope you will discover what joy can be found in giving these stories to others, whatever the age, and how it enriches the depth of your Bible study and faith.

Introduction

The Importance of Stories

"Children, come join me for the story," the storyteller beckoned, with arms open. Girls and boys hurried forward to get a spot next to a friend. Some children hesitated, holding a parent's hand, as they walked slowly to the front of the sanctuary. When everyone was settled, the storyteller began, "Long, long ago, even before Jesus was born. . . ." You could feel the congregation, adults and children, relax and settle in to hear the story. A good story, told well, has something for everyone, from age four to ninety-four and beyond. Certainly the Bible is filled with good stories. And worship is an occasion for all generations to hear the story together. Hearing the story together is no small thing, for we Christians are a storied people, and hearing it at the same time and in the same space brings all generations together.

Many reasons are given for including a children's sermon or time with the children in the order of worship. At one end of the spectrum, it functions as a way to transition the children from the worship service to their church school classes. In that case, the little talk or story may have nothing to do with anything else that takes place in worship or in what children do in their church school classes. Too often, it is a story or talk that is prepared hurriedly and ends with a moral, one that is often beyond the understanding of the children.

But let's back up for a moment. Why is storytelling of any kind important? Stories—family stories, community stories, national stories, faith stories—are how we pass values from one generation to the next. These stories tell us who we are and what is important to our families, our tribes, our nations, our faith communities. These stories bind us together. In this same way, Bible stories bind us together as the people of God. They tell us who we are and whose we are. They help us see God at work in our world. They incorporate us into the body of Christ. And stories begin to work this wonder when we are very, very young. What better time, then, to tell Bible stories on a regular basis than when the faith community is gathered in its most unique and faithful act, the worship of God.

When the Bible story that is told matches the sermon text, the story provides an entry point into the sermon for adults and children as they ponder the story and how it is proclaimed in the sermon. Repetition of the story as it is told and as it is read from the Bible reinforces the text, its structure and plot, and need not be a concern for worship planners.

When that text is also the passage studied in church school, whether for children or all ages—which is possible when using a lectionary-based curriculum such as *Feasting on the Word*—the possibilities for faith formation are multiplied. But these optimal conditions are not necessary to nurture faith through telling Bible stories in worship.

The ultimate goal is to tell the Bible story so the listeners' imaginations and hearts catch fire, as happened to the disciples on the road to Emmaus when Jesus told the stories of the prophets. Bible stories help us recognize Jesus and meet the God who sent him to us.

Another reason for telling Bible stories in worship is to free these stories from the page. When Moses spoke to "all Israel" as the people were about to enter the promised land without him, he told them that everyone was responsible for teaching the children, and this was no small thing "but their very life." Every adult in the church has some responsibility for telling the story to the next generation. Indeed, the congregation promises that to each infant baptized. When the story is told in worship, adults have a model to follow. They find that it's just fine to laugh at a humorous detail or to wonder what happened next. They also learn that they don't have to include every word or get everything right. After all, this is how Bible stories were passed from generation to generation, by word of mouth from one person to the next. Not every adult will tell the story to the congregation but might tell it to one or two children or grandchildren.

Everyone is a storyteller. Think about it. When you find a bargain at the mall and phone a friend to tell about it, you are telling a story. When a child asks, "What was school like when you were in second grade, Grandmom?" and you tell about your second grade classroom, you are telling a story. Stories help us know each other, our dreams, our fears, and our joys. We may not all be comfortable telling stories before a group, whether children or adults, but we are all storytellers, and some of us are called to be storytellers of the church's story to the congregation, the whole congregation.

One more thought about telling Bible stories in the service of worship. If you have heard StoryCorps on a public broadcasting station, you know that personal stories can delight, enlighten, heal, and bridge gaps in relationships. David Isay, the originator of StoryCorps, describes the stories collected as conversations in sacred space.[1] No, they are not recorded in a religious building, but the stories are the meeting of two souls with a facilitator, whose task is to listen, listen intently, to bear witness to the story and storyteller. Perhaps the adults in the congregation are the silent witnesses to the story when it is told in worship. If that is the case, adults are included in the audience for the story. It's not for children only.

For all of these reasons about the importance of story and the place Bible stories have in nurturing the faith in all ages, perhaps we ought to think of the time when children come forward as a time to tell the Bible story in worship rather than a children's sermon or time with the children. The story is for everyone present; it's just that the children get a front row seat. It's a story, not a sermon. Thinking of this worship element as a children's sermon has fostered too many pious talks that end with a moral. Or children are subjected to an object lesson before they are able to comprehend metaphor, and they become fixated on the object. Occasionally something said leading up to the story distracts children from even hearing the story. Many years ago, a person giving the children's sermon began by telling the children that he had hit a deer on the way to church. A mother reported later that her boys could talk about nothing else the rest of the day. Did they hear the message of the children's sermon? Probably not. Tell the story. Tell it with all the enthusiasm and delight that you can muster so that God's Word is given to each person in the sanctuary.

1. David Isay, "Transcript for David Isay—Listening as an Act of Love," *On Being*, April 17, 2014, http://www.onbeing.org/program/dave-isay-the-everyday-art-of-listening /transcript/6274.

Preparing the Story

This book provides a story for telling in worship based on one of the Year A lectionary texts for each Sunday, from the first Sunday in Advent to Reign of Christ/Christ the King Sunday (the end of the church year), as well as a story for Christmas. Also included are four stories for special times in the congregation's life. These stories are about five minutes long.

To prepare to tell a story provided here, read both the story and text that is the basis for the story. Adapt the story so the style and the words or phrases are comfortable for you. Don't try to memorize it word for word. You are *telling* the story, not reciting it.

Practice telling the story over and over. Tell it to a mirror, to your pet, to anyone who will listen. As you tell it again and again, you will find phrases and word combinations that are natural for you, but keep the language simple and appropriate for children. Then it is appropriate for those adults who are listening intently too. Using language and concepts the children will understand doesn't make it boring for youth and adults. A story told with enthusiasm will draw in the entire congregation.

As you practice telling the story, notice how your arms or head move naturally to the emotions or content of the story. Perhaps you stand tall and strong to emphasize the power of Jesus when he calms the storm. Or you might shield your eyes and look into the distance as you tell about the lost sheep. If you find motions difficult, pantomime the story, using actions and no words. You may discover some natural movements in the process.

With a longer story, you may find it helpful to get the scenes firmly in your mind. One method is to outline the story and remember the outline by memorizing the opening words for each scene.

Have the opening and closing sentences firmly in mind. This is an exception to telling, not memorizing the story. Knowing how you will begin and end relieves some of the stress. Being prepared with a strong concluding sentence will keep the story from drifting away from you and the listeners.

When telling the Bible story, sound practice suggests that you do not ask a question of the children. Someone will answer you, and more often than not the answer provokes a chuckle from the congregation. Too many children have been hurt by that ripple of laughter, because they answer with all seriousness. The better road is to avoid asking questions.

Occasionally, a child will ask a question in the middle of the story. For example, a girl of about seven asked, "What does 'getting even' mean?" The story was about the rules from God in Leviticus 19, and the storyteller said, "When someone is mean to you, don't try to get even." The storyteller, in a sentence, explained "getting even." The child responded, "Oh, I thought maybe it was getting everything right." One can understand why a child might think that. Such distractions and other kinds will happen. Take them in stride and try to keep your focus.

Telling the Story to the Whole Congregation

Everyone comes along when a story is told well. And most people, with practice, can learn to tell a story well. Here are some things to consider:

Stand facing the congregation with the children facing you. Sitting in the congregation and listening to a disembodied story, when you know the storyteller is using motions and movement, is distracting. Encourage the children to look at you by saying something like, "Sit so I can see your eyes."

Look at the children and focus on one child who is eagerly waiting to hear the story for a moment. Then begin with the opening sentence you carefully crafted.

When the story includes a quoted section from the Bible, as in a letter from the New Testament, write or type the quote. Roll it up like a scroll and open it to read during the story. Or place your paraphrase in the Bible and open it to read the paraphrase. Use a Bible that the children will recognize so they know that what you are reading is from this very book.

While motions and movement can contribute to the excitement and action of the story, try to keep your own actions to a well-selected minimum. Too much movement is distracting from the story. Constant pacing back and forth makes the listeners dizzy.

At the end of the story, after you have said that carefully prepared closing sentence, hold the gaze of a child who has been listening intently for just a moment before praying.

Enjoy telling the story. What a wonderful gift you are giving to each person who is listening, whether this is the first time a child has heard it or the adults know it backwards and forwards. But that's the wonderful thing, the story you tell may invite adults familiar with it to look at the words from another angle. The wondrous thing about the Bible is that there is always more to say and ponder.

Writing Other Bible Stories
to Tell to the Congregation

Sometimes the lectionary texts aren't what you want or the sermon text is not from the lectionary. Then the storyteller is responsible for writing a story. The story "Queen Vashti" (p. xvii) was written for that reason, since Esther 1 never appears in the Revised Common Lectionary. Once the text is chosen, follow these steps.

1. Read at least one commentary on the passage. Look for interpretations or information that will guide how you approach the story. For example, if the story text is from Philippians, explain that Paul wrote this letter to the church in Philippi while he was in prison. For the story of Queen Vashti, notice how the story begins because it is difficult to date the book of Esther and because it was certainly written long after the events it records.

2. Read the text in several translations, including one with a limited English vocabulary (CEV or Good News). Notice how the translations differ and where they are alike or similar. If you are the preacher and the storyteller, steps one and two will serve for the sermon preparation and the story preparation. The other steps may also help you move into the story as you begin your sermon preparation. Be open to the possibility.

3. Tell the story to yourself. If you aren't sure of the sequence, just keep going. This will help you establish a rhythm for the story and identify the parts of it that are important and memorable. Go back to the text and see what you missed or added.

4. Write the story as you would like to tell it. One of the

most difficult things about writing the story is selecting words that convey meaning to the children. Bible stories are not occasions to show off your vocabulary or clever phrasing, for the children or the adults. Paraphrase sections of speeches or letters you want to include. This is a rough draft. Pay no attention to grammatical details, misspelled words, or sentence structure.

5. Compare your written story to the text. Add missing details that are important to the story. Are there details that will enliven the storytelling that you can add without compromising the text? Check on the sequence of events. Is your story faithful to the text and what you know about it from reading the commentary? If you compare "Queen Vashti" to Esther 1, you will soon notice details that are not part of the story, such as the names of the king's eunuchs and the details about the drinking party. Yet the essence of the story and Vashti's role in setting up the necessity for a new queen come through clearly.

Generally, you can omit details that are inappropriate for children without damaging the intent of the story. For example, in Year B, the Gospel lectionary text for Proper 20 is Mark 9:30–37. Verses 30–32 are Jesus' prediction of his death, while verses 33–37 tell of Jesus' conversation with the disciples about who is the greatest. When preparing the story for telling in worship, base the story on verses 33–37. Omitting the first three verses doesn't change the story of when Jesus and the disciples reach Capernaum. When you look at that text carefully, it is two stories. As a rule of thumb, keep to one story for this moment in worship.

6. The opening and closing sentences of the story are especially important. Write the opening sentence carefully

to get the attention of the listeners right away. Look at "Queen Vashti" and notice how the opening sentence tells the listeners that this is a story from the Old Testament, a story that Jesus may have heard as a child. The words "A very long time ago, way, way longer than anyone here can remember" draws listeners in to hear how the story unfolds. The closing sentence is just as important because this may help the listeners remember the story and helps you draw the story to a close. This is not a moral or explanation of the story; it is the conclusion of the story. Look at "Queen Vashti." The closing sentence encourages the listeners to ponder the story on their own and clearly marks that this is the end of Vashti's story. Indeed, nothing more is said about her in the book of Esther. If you read Esther 1, Vashti's story doesn't have an ending. The closing sentence of the story doesn't provide an ending either, but it does provide a way to end the story being told.

7. Now you are ready to rehearse. As suggested earlier, rehearsal of the story will make all the difference in your role as storyteller. Tell the story aloud often. Let your body move naturally to the story's emotions and content. If you find motions difficult, try pantomiming the story or if you enjoy drawing, sketch the story in scenes. You may discover some natural movements in the process. Examine vocabulary and figures of speech to be sure you haven't strayed from language accessible to children. And memorize the opening and closing sentences so you have them firmly in mind. Incorporate them into the story so they sound natural.

Queen Vashti

A very long time ago, way, way longer than anyone here can remember, King Asheruerus ruled over all the land from Ethiopia to India. He wanted to show all the important men of those countries just how rich and important he was, so he had a big feast, a banquet. He invited the councilors of the court, the generals of the army, and the governors of the lands. This feast was not just for one night, or two or three nights, or even ten nights. It went on for 180 nights.

When that big party ended, the king had another party just for the men of Susa where his royal palace was. He held it in the courtyard of the palace. The courtyard had big marble pillars. They were draped with fine blue cloth, held in place with silver rings. The floor sparkled with mother-of-pearl and beautiful colored stones.

While the king was entertaining the men, Queen Vashti had a party for the women. It was in another part of the palace. I think they were far enough apart that one party didn't bother the other one.

On the seventh night of his party, the king was feeling pretty good and very important. He sent seven servants with a message for Queen Vashti.

The servants said to Queen Vashti, "A message from the king. 'Come to me. Wear your royal crown so all the men of Susa will see what a beautiful queen I have.'"

Queen Vashti thought for a moment. It was dangerous not to obey the king's command, but she was entertaining her own guests. She sent this message back to the king: "I will not come."

Was the king angry when he got her message! The more he thought about it, the angrier he got. "What must be done with Queen Vashti?" he asked the seven councilors of the court. They huddled together and whispered. "If the queen does not obey the king, our wives will find out and they won't pay any attention to us. We cannot have that!" So they said to the king, "Send a royal decree to all the land. Say that because Queen Vashti did not obey your command to come to you, she is never able to come to you again; and get a new queen."

The king smiled. He liked that idea. In fact, the more he thought about it, the more he liked it. So a decree went out to all the land, from India to Ethiopia: "Because Queen Vashti refused to obey the king, she can never come before him again."

Now some people feel sorry for Vashti, but I think she was a brave and intelligent woman. Although she was no longer queen, she still lived in the palace, and I think she rather liked it that way.

A Word about the Lectionary

During Ordinary Time, or the season after Pentecost, the Revised Common Lectionary offers two streams, or tracks, in the readings: semicontinuous and complementary streams. Each stream uses the same Epistle and Gospel reading, but the Old Testament and Psalms lections are different. The semicontinuous track allows congregations to read continually through a book of Scripture from week to week. In the complementary track, the Old Testament readings are chosen to relate to (or complement) the Gospel reading of the day. In both cases, the psalm is understood as a response to the Old Testament reading. This book provides a story for each week during Ordinary time, no matter which track a church uses. Many weeks include a story from each track.

Since the numbering of the Sundays after Pentecost varies from year to year, the designation of "Proper" is used here, as it is in the *Feasting on the Word* commentaries and Worship Companions. It can be confusing to navigate the various ways churches designate Sundays; a handy resource for viewing all those labels in one place can be found at http://lectionary.library.vanderbilt.edu/, a user-friendly site provided to the public by Vanderbilt University.

❧ LECTIONARY DATES ❧

Words of Hope
Isaiah 2:1–5

In the time of Isaiah long, long before Jesus was born, God's people in Jerusalem needed to hear God's message of peace. *What could they hope for?* wondered the people. They knew war was coming to Jerusalem. How could they prepare for it?

King Ahaz wanted words from God's prophet, Isaiah. This is what Isaiah told the king and the people:

> "In the days to come,
>> God's mountain will be higher than any other
>> mountain.
> "People of many nations will say,
> 'Let's go up on God's mountain
>> where the God of Israel can teach us
>> so we can follow God's ways.
>> Then we can walk in God's paths.'
>> "God will be in charge.
> God will settle arguments and fights.
> "Then no one will need swords or other things for
>> fighting,

and all the swords can be made into peaceful
   things,
   like plows for the fields.
"Then one country will not fight any other country.
   No one will be taught how to fight wars.
"Come, God's people,
   let's walk in God's light!"

   These were good words for King Ahaz and for God's people, don't you think? God is in charge! An important message
for us, too, as we begin the season of Advent.

Prayer: God of hope, we will try to remember not to worry,
because we know you are in charge. Amen.

Words of Peace
Isaiah 11:1–10

The people of Judah were afraid. They worried that war would start any day. But Isaiah, God's prophet who spoke of hope, had more words from God for them. Isaiah told them that it was true that their nation would be destroyed by another nation, a powerful nation. But God had good words for them too. Here is what Isaiah told them. Listen for words of peace.

"Wait for someone wise and strong,
    who will come from the family of Jesse.
"This one will worship and serve God.
    This one will be filled with God's Spirit.
"This one will judge fairly.
    Imagine how the world might be then.
"The lion and the lamb will live together.
    So will the leopard and the young goat.
"The calf and the young lion will eat side by side,
    and a child, a little child, will lead them.
"The cow and the bear will eat in the same field,
    while their calves and cubs nap together.
    Lions will eat straw like the oxen.

"A baby will play by a snake's hole and not be hurt.
"No creature will damage anything on God's holy
      mountain.
"The earth will be filled with the words and ways
      of God
    as water covers the sea.
"On that day, the one from Jesse's family will stand,
a signal to all people. All nations will look for this
one, whose place will be glorious."

Imagine that! All these animals living together in peace. In Advent we remember these words from God as we wait for Jesus, who was from Jesse's family, too.

Prayer: God of peace, your picture of peace fills our hearts and dreams as we wait for the one you sent into the world. Amen.

Words That Question
Matthew 11:2–11

Many years after the prophet Isaiah gave God's words of hope and peace to the people of Judah, another prophet of God, John the baptizer, told people to return to God's ways and be baptized. Some people became John's followers and learned from him.

When John heard that Jesus was healing people who were sick and teaching people about God, he sent his followers to check Jesus out.

John's followers caught up with Jesus and asked him, "Are you the one from God for whom we have waited for so long, or must we keep on waiting and watching for someone else?"

Jesus answered, "Go back to John. Tell him what you have seen and what you have heard. People who were blind can see. People who could not walk can walk. People who were deaf can hear. People who were sick are strong and healthy. People who are poor have heard good news."

The followers of John the baptizer left to tell him what they had seen and heard. Jesus said to the crowd of people with him, "Why did you go to the Jordan River to be baptized by John? You went because John is God's prophet. But John is more than a prophet. Another prophet, many years before

John, had this message from God: 'I'm sending my messenger, who will prepare the way.' That messenger is John. He prepared the way for me."

In Advent, the church remembers this story as we prepare to welcome Jesus.

Prayer: Loving God, we join John the baptizer in preparing the way for the arrival of the one you sent, Jesus. Amen.

Words That Surprise
Matthew 1:18–25

The story of the birth of Jesus with shepherds and angels is found only in the Gospel of Luke. This is how the story of Jesus' birth is told in the Gospel of Matthew.

The young woman Mary was engaged to be married to Joseph. Everything had been planned by their families. But before they were married, God's Holy Spirit came to Mary and told her, "You will have a baby, God's baby."

Mary had to tell Joseph, who did not think this was good news. Joseph was a faithful Jew, but he didn't want to make Mary the talk of the village. Finally, he decided that he would call off the engagement quietly. Perhaps everyone would forget about it.

But before this happened, Joseph had a dream. In this dream, an angel of God came to him. The angel said, "Joseph, son of David of the house of Jesse, listen carefully. Take Mary as your wife. Don't be afraid to do this, because the baby she will have is from God's Holy Spirit. When she has this baby boy, name him Jesus. This baby will save God's people from their sins."

When Joseph woke up the next day, he did exactly what the angel of God had said to him. He married Mary. Some months later, she had a baby boy and Joseph named him Jesus.

All of this happened because the prophet Isaiah said it would (see Isaiah 7:14):

> "A woman will have a baby boy. He will be called Immanuel,* which means 'God is with us.'"

The season of Advent is almost over. Soon we will celebrate the birth of this baby boy Jesus. This is a sign that God is with us, Immanuel.

Prayer: God, we are counting the days until we celebrate the birth of Jesus. Send your Spirit to us then too. Amen.

---

*For the child who questions the discrepancy of names, explain that *Jesus* was a common name at the time and also means "God saves."

In the Fields
Luke 2:1–14(15–20)

Mary and Joseph were among many others going to Bethlehem because Caesar Augustus had said that all the people had to go to their hometowns to be added to the tax list. But Mary and Joseph were traveling slowly because Mary was soon to have a baby. I hope she rode a donkey, but it doesn't say that in the Gospel of Luke, just that they traveled from Nazareth to Bethlehem, a trip of sixty or seventy miles . . . walking on foot as most travelers did then.

When they got to Bethlehem, all the guest rooms were filled. The only place they found to spend the night was in a room where the cattle stayed. That night they were barely settled when Mary gave birth to a baby boy. She wrapped him snugly in cloths and laid him in a manger, where the food for the cattle was placed.

In a field outside Bethlehem, a field that Mary and Joseph may have passed that day, shepherds were taking care of their sheep. Without any warning, an angel of God appeared and God's glory shone all around them. They jumped and hid their faces.

"Don't be afraid," said the angel. "I have good news for you. Tonight your Savior was born in Bethlehem. This baby is Christ the Lord. Go, you will find the baby wrapped snugly in cloths and sleeping in a manger."

Then the sky was filled with angels singing, "Glory to God! Peace on earth to everyone who pleases God."

As quickly as they came, all the angels were gone. The shepherds said, "Let's go to Bethlehem and see this baby."

Off they went! After they saw the baby in the manger and Mary and Joseph, they left. But they told everyone they met what they had seen and heard.

Prayer: God of surprises and wonder, today we celebrate with the shepherds that our Savior is born. Glory to God! Amen.

A Sudden Trip to Egypt
Matthew 2:13–23

Some wise men called magi, who lived in far-off lands in the East, saw a new star in the sky. They believed this was a sign that there was a new king for Israel and decided to find out for themselves.

When they came to Jerusalem, they weren't sure where to go. They asked King Herod, "Where can we find the new king of Israel?"

This wasn't good news for King Herod. A new king would be big trouble for him. But King Herod was clever and sly. He asked his advisors where a new king would be found. They said, "Bethlehem."

When King Herod gave this answer to the magi, he said, "When you find this new king, come tell me where he is so I can visit him too."

The magi did find the child Jesus in Bethlehem. When they were ready to return to King Herod in Jerusalem, they had a dream. In this dream, an angel of God told them not to go to Jerusalem but to go home a different way.

After some days, King Herod realized that the magi were not going to tell him where the new king of Israel was. He was angry, and he plotted to get rid of this new king.

About the same time, Joseph had a dream. An angel of God said to him, "Get up. Take the child and his mother. Go to Egypt. It is not safe for your child here. Stay there until I say you can return safely."

In the middle of the night, Joseph got up. He woke Mary and told her about the dream. Immediately, they packed up all they had and took Jesus to Egypt where he would be safe.

After King Herod died, Joseph had another dream, and the angel of God told him of Herod's death. But before they left Egypt, Joseph heard that Herod's son was king, and he was as mean and clever as his father. So Joseph took Jesus and Mary to Nazareth in Galilee where they would be safe from the king in Jerusalem.

Prayer: Awesome God, angels may not speak to us in dreams, but we are sure that you watch over us too. Amen.

The Light
John 1:(1–9)10–18

The writer, we'll call him John, was deep in thought. How could he tell people about Jesus Christ so they would understand what a special person he was? He wanted them to get how closely Jesus and God were tied together.

Finally, he started to write: "In the beginning was Jesus. Jesus was with God. Jesus was God. Jesus was with God in the beginning."

"Well, that's a start," he muttered to himself. "This is hard."

Then he wrote: "Everything was created by Jesus and God. God and Jesus gave life to everything that was created. The life was light for all the world, for all people."

"Light!" Now he was on a roll. "Jesus is that light. The light of Jesus came into the darkness, and nothing could put it out. John the baptizer told people to believe in the light. Some people did, and some people didn't. But the people who did believe welcomed the light of Jesus."

John stopped to read what was written. Then he wrote: "Then Jesus came to earth, looking just like an ordinary person. Jesus lived among ordinary people too. Now we have seen his glory, the glory of God, full of grace and truth."

This writer we call John had begun his story about the good news of Jesus. Truly, it is unlike every other story in the Bible, and it tells us how special Jesus was and is.

Prayer: God of grace and truth, it is hard for us to imagine how special Jesus is, but we are thankful that people wrote about him so we can read and think about him and you. Amen.

You Can't Imagine
Matthew 2:1–12

The magi, sometimes called the wise men, were home again. It had been a long journey to Jerusalem, then to Bethlehem, and back home. These men, the Gospel of Matthew doesn't tell us how many, had a story to tell!

Perhaps they told family and friends like this:

We followed that new star in the sky all the way to Jerusalem. Then it was hard to figure out exactly where to go. We also thought it was a good idea to speak with the king there so he wouldn't wonder why our caravan had come. So we went to the palace to introduce ourselves to King Herod. He seemed very friendly.

"Where is the new baby who is to be the king of the Jews?" we asked, because our study of the stars led us to believe that was the meaning of the star we were following.

King Herod looked puzzled, so we explained, "We study the night skies. We saw this star in the east, which we believe to be a sign that a new king has been born. We have followed the star all this way to honor him."

At first, King Herod looked upset, but he quickly covered up his feelings and said, "Let me talk with the chief priests and those who are expert in such things. I'll get back to you."

The king and the experts stood far enough from us that we could not hear what they were saying, but it looked like King Herod was worried.

When the king returned to us, he said in a whisper, "When did you first see this star in the sky?"

We told him. Then he said, "The baby is to be born in Bethlehem in Judea, for the prophet has said this. Go and find this new baby king. When you do, come back and tell me where he is so I can honor him too."

Bethlehem was not far from Jerusalem, so we followed the star until it led us to a simple house, a surprising place for a king, even a baby king. But we took the gifts we had brought with us from the camel packs and went to the house. There we found the child and his mother. We knelt before him and gave him our presents—gold, frankincense, and myrrh.

We planned to return to Jerusalem the next day, but that night we were warned in a dream not to go to Jerusalem. Apparently King Herod was not as nice as we thought he was. So we came home by another route that didn't go anywhere close to Jerusalem, and here we are today!

Prayer: Gracious God, the magi remind us that you are special to people all over the world. Amen.

Jesus at the Jordan River
Matthew 3:13–17

Jesus was on his way to the Jordan River. He knew that John the baptizer was there every day, preaching about God and baptizing people. People from all over came to hear John tell them to turn around and follow God's ways. If they agreed, he baptized them in the Jordan River. Even the Jewish leaders from Jerusalem came to see what John was doing.

Before Jesus could see John, he heard John call, "Change. Turn back to God! Live new lives! The kingdom of heaven is near!"

But if anyone asked who he was, John said, "I am preparing the way for someone coming from God who will be greater. I baptize with water, but the one God sends will baptize with the Holy Spirit."

When Jesus got to where John was baptizing people, he got in line with everyone else. When he was next, John stopped. "I should be baptized by you, but you come to be baptized by me?"

"Baptize me now," said Jesus. "This is important to God's plan for me."

What could John say to that? So he baptized Jesus just like he baptized everyone else. He dipped Jesus down into the river until the water covered him.

But Jesus' baptism wasn't like the baptism of everyone else. As Jesus came up out of the water, the Spirit of God came to him in the shape of a bird, a dove. And that wasn't all! A voice from the skies said, "This is my Son. I love him dearly. He makes me happy."

The story of the baptism of Jesus is found in all four Gospels—Matthew, Mark, Luke, and John. That means it is a very important story. The story today was based on the Gospel of Matthew.

Prayer: Loving God, your words of love and happiness to Jesus remind us that you love us too. Thank you. Amen.

The Next Day
John 1:29–42

One day when John was baptizing in the Jordan River, he saw Jesus coming toward him. The next day John saw Jesus again and said, "He is the Lamb of God who takes away the sins of the world. I have been getting people ready for him to come. He is much more important than I am. When I baptized him yesterday, I saw the Holy Spirit come to him. It was amazing!"

Later the same day John was talking with two of his followers. He saw Jesus walking by him again. "See him? He is the Lamb of God!"

John's followers knew from John's teachings that this was important. They left John and went after Jesus.

When Jesus saw that they were following him, he asked, "What do you want?"

They asked, "Where are you staying?"

"Come and see," said Jesus.

So the two followers of John did. They stayed with Jesus all day. One of them was Andrew. When he left Jesus, he went to find his brother Simon. Andrew was excited. "Simon," he said, "we have found the Messiah, the one sent from God."

Then Andrew took Simon to see Jesus. Jesus looked at

Simon and said, "You are Simon, son of John" (but not John the baptizer). "I will call you Peter." From then on, Simon was also called Peter. The brothers, Andrew and Peter, became two of the first followers of Jesus. John's follower who was with Andrew became a follower of Jesus too.

Prayer: Holy God, we want to be followers of Jesus too. Amen.

Words to Help
1 Corinthians 1:10–18

Paul sat at his writing table, his head in his hands. How could he help his friends in Corinth? Paul had lived in Corinth for a year and a half, teaching the Christians there and helping them start a church. He knew the people, and he loved them as a father loves his children.

He was upset that news had come to him that the people in the Corinth church were fighting among themselves. Some people were saying they were better and more important than others.

Paul couldn't go see them, so he was writing a letter to them. He began:

> "From Paul, an apostle of the Lord Jesus Christ.
> "To God's church in Corinth.
> "Grace and peace to you from God and Jesus Christ."

Then Paul stopped. What could he say so they would stop arguing and fighting? How could he help them remember that they were one in Jesus Christ? He thought and thought. He shook his head, and he thought some more. He wrote:

"I thank God for you every day. I ask you, brothers and sisters, in the name of Jesus Christ, to stop arguing with one another. Cooperate and agree so you have the same mind and goal. I came to you to preach the good news of Jesus."

Paul stretched his back. He had more to say, but this was a good start.

Paul's letter to the church in Corinth is in our Bible. It is called the First Letter to the Corinthians. We read and try to follow his words today too.

Prayer: God, help us follow the words of Paul written to the church in Corinth so that we cooperate and show our love for you. In Jesus' name, we pray. Amen.

Filled with Joy
Matthew 5:1–12

Jesus and the disciples, his best friends, traveled all over Galilee, to Judea and beyond the Jordan River. Crowds of people came to hear Jesus teach about God's love. Sometimes they brought sick people for him to heal.

On this day, Jesus wanted some quiet time away from all the people. He took the disciples up a mountain, where he could talk with them alone. Jesus sat down, and the disciples gathered around him. They listened carefully as he said to them:

> "People who feel hopeless will be filled with joy;
>   the kingdom of heaven is theirs.
> "People who are sad about many things will be
>   filled with joy;
>   they will be glad again.
> "People who do not brag will be filled with joy;
>   they will be given the earth.
> "People who long to do what is right will be filled
>   with joy;
>   they will be generous and fair.

"People who show kindness and forgiveness will be
    filled with joy;
  kindness and forgiveness will be shown them.
"People who live faithfully will be filled with joy;
    they will see God.
"People who work for peace will be filled with joy;
    they will be called God's children.
"People who are teased and bullied because they
      are faithful to God's ways,
    rejoice and be happy for your reward in heaven
      is great!"

Words like these are in the Gospel of Matthew, and we call them the Beatitudes.

Prayer: Gracious God, Jesus' words fill us with joy. We give you praise and thanks. In Jesus' name, we pray. Amen.

Two Examples
Matthew 5:13–20

Jesus sat down on the side of the mountain. The disciples sat facing him. They were ready to listen to his teaching.

Jesus had invited each disciple to travel with him. He knew each one of them. Now he looked at each of them, thinking about all that he wanted to tell them. He said, "You are the salt of the earth. But when salt is no longer salty, it isn't any good. It doesn't make food taste better, and it doesn't preserve food. It's good for nothing."

He paused and looked at his friends. Did they understand what he was telling them? Jesus pointed to them and said, "You are the light of the world. A city on the top of a hill can't be hidden. Travelers see it from every side. When you light a lamp, you don't cover it with a bucket. No, you put that lamp in the middle of the room so you can see in every corner."

Some heads nodded. The disciples understood about lamps.

Jesus continued, "Just like that lamp, let your light, God's light, shine brightly so everyone can see it. Then people will know what good things God has done and praise God."

The disciples smiled. Jesus said, "God's law is still important. Pay attention to it and you will be called great in the kingdom of heaven."

Prayer: Good God, with your help, we will let your light shine through us every day. In Jesus's name, we pray. Amen.

A Big Choice
Deuteronomy 30:15–20

It had taken forty years, but the people of Israel were almost to the land that God promised them. So much happened during those years, but I don't have time to tell those stories today. Moses had led them, with God's help, every step of the forty years. And Moses had some words from God for them now.

He gathered the people together and told them what God expected them to do. The people shouted, "Yes, yes!"

Moses said, "You are to follow God and live in God's ways so other people will know that you belong to God."

The people shouted, "Yes, yes!"

Moses said, "God's laws are for you and for your children and they are not too hard for you to obey."

The people shouted, "Yes, yes!"

Moses had one more choice for the people to make, a big choice, an important choice. He said to the people:

"Look at me! Listen carefully! You have the choice to live with God or to live without God. To live with God means that you will live in God's ways, obeying God's word. You will keep God's commandments. If you choose to live with God, God will bless you. To live without God means you will not pay attention to God's ways or God's commandments. It you say 'no' to God and worship other gods, it will not be good for you.

"So now, this very minute, choose life with God! What do you say?"

The story ends there in the Bible. Moses goes on to tell the people more of God's words. But what do you think the people said? (*Expect a chorus of "Yes, yes!"*)

Prayer: God of life, today we choose to live with you, to live in your ways, and to obey your commandments. Thank you for life. Amen.

Help Your Neighbors
Leviticus 19:1–2, 9–18

During the forty long years the Israelites took to get from Egypt to their new home, the home God had planned for them, they had some rough times. When they were slaves in Egypt, the pharaoh made all the decisions: when they worked, what they ate, where they lived. Everything was decided by the pharaoh. Now they were free, but sometimes they forgot how to live as God's people. God had chosen Moses as their leader; God and Moses often met so God could give Moses words for the people to help them remember.

Some messages from God were about how to worship God, so those words were for the priests. Some messages were about children, so those words were for mothers, fathers, and all people who care for children. Some messages were for everyone. All of the messages began the same way. God would tell Moses to say to the people, "You must be holy, because I the LORD your God am holy." Then came special words from God.

These messages, words from God, are in the Old Testament, or Hebrew Scriptures, in our Bible. The words for today come from the book of Leviticus: "You shall be holy, for I the LORD your God am holy."

Then Moses continued:

"When you cut down or harvest your fields of wheat or barley, leave some standing around the edges of the field. When you pick your grapes, leave some on the vines and don't pick up the grapes that have fallen to the ground. The wheat and barley around the edges of the fields and the grapes left on the vine and on the ground are for people who are poor or strangers who have come to live in your land. I am the LORD your God.

"Don't steal or lie. Be kind to your neighbors. Pay your workers every day. Say kind things about people who are deaf and clear the way for someone who is blind. I am the LORD your God.

"Treat everyone fairly for no one is more important than anyone else. Speak only the truth about people. Help your neighbors when they are in trouble.

"Love everyone and don't stay mad at anyone. No, love your neighbor as you love yourself. I am the LORD your God."

Perhaps the last part, "love your neighbor as you love yourself," sounds familiar to you. Many, many years later, someone asked Jesus about the most important commandment from God. Jesus said, "'Love God with all your heart, soul, strength and mind, and love your neighbor as yourself." And that is how God's people still try to live today.

Prayer: God of love, this week we will work hard to love our neighbors as we love ourselves. Amen.

Not to Worry
Matthew 6:24–34

Day after day, Jesus taught crowds of people about God's ways and God's love. People couldn't seem to get enough of his stories, and Jesus was eager to teach everyone who came to him.

In the crowd were rich people and people who were very poor. Some people were old and some people were young. But sometimes Jesus wanted to teach only the twelve disciples he had chosen to travel with him. He knew that if his teaching about God were to reach more people, his friends would have to teach about God too.

On this day, Jesus was alone with the twelve disciples. It wasn't often that he could talk just with them, so he took advantage of the time to teach them. He taught them how to pray to God. He told them how to behave and how to live. He said, "Don't worry. Don't worry about your life. Don't worry about what you will wear or what you will eat. Life is more than clothes and food."

Jesus pointed to the sky where birds were circling as free as could be. "Look at those birds," said Jesus. "They don't plant gardens or fields of grain, yet God makes sure they have food to eat. You know that you are worth more than these birds to God. And worry won't add one minute to your life."

Jesus pointed to their clothes and said, "Why worry about your clothes? See those beautiful flowers, those lilies growing over there? They are dressed as beautifully as any queen or king, even King Solomon. If God makes the field beautiful with flowers like these, which bloom only for a few days, won't God do the same for you?"

The disciples watched the birds and admired the flowers, but Jesus wasn't finished. "So don't worry. Don't ask 'What are we going to eat?' or 'What are we going to wear?' Other people who are not God's people worry about these things. But we want most of all to live in God's ways and love; then everything will be given to us. So stop worrying about tomorrow. Let tomorrow worry about itself."

The disciples, who had left everything behind but the clothes on their backs when they chose to follow Jesus, had a lot to ponder.

Prayer: Caring God, remind us every day that we do not need to worry, but instead to remember to live in your ways. In Jesus' name, we pray. Amen.

A Strong Foundation
Matthew 7:21–29

Each Gospel—Matthew, Mark, Luke, and John—has a special way of telling the story of Jesus. Matthew includes the travels of the magi who were looking for the new king of the Jews. Luke reminds readers often that Jesus is headed to Jerusalem.

If there is one message that stands out in the Gospel of Matthew, it is that we are to live as Jesus taught. Saying "I believe" is not enough. To make this point to the crowd one day, Jesus told this short but powerful story.

"When you listen to what I tell you and do what I say, you are like a wise builder who built a house on a foundation of rock. A storm came. Heavy rain and strong winds beat against the house. Windows rattled and boards creaked. But the house did not fall down because it was built on a strong foundation.

"A foolish builder built a house on sand. A storm came. Heavy rain and strong winds beat against the house. Windows rattled and boards creaked. And the house fell down, completely destroyed because the foolish man had not built on a strong foundation."

34

At the end of the story, the crowd was speechless. This man Jesus taught them with authority, not like their religious leaders taught.

Prayer: Guiding God, open our hearts and heads to hear Jesus and do as he teaches us to do. Amen.

Listen, but Don't Tell
Matthew 17:1–9

Every year on this Sunday, which is called Transfiguration Sunday, we hear the same gospel story. *Transfiguration* means that something changes in the way it looks. Listen for what or who changes in this story.

Jesus and the disciples had been traveling around Galilee for quite some time. Crowds came to Jesus with people to be healed and to hear him teach about the kingdom of God. But on this day, Jesus asked three of the disciples—Peter, James, and his brother John—to walk to the top of a mountain so they were far away from the other disciples.

They assumed, I imagine, that Jesus was going up the mountain to pray to God and wanted them to pray too. But when they got to a level place where they could sit and pray, Jesus' body became as bright as the sun in the middle of the day. His clothes sparkled like a bright light.

Suddenly Moses and Elijah, prophets of long ago, were standing next to Jesus, and the three of them were talking. Peter said to Jesus, "It's a good thing we came with you. Do you want me to make shelters, one for Moses, one for Elijah, and one for you?"

Before Peter finished his question, a bright cloud came over the mountain, covering everyone there. From the cloud, a voice said, "This is my Son. I love him dearly. He makes me happy. Listen to him."

When the voice from the cloud began to speak, Peter, James, and John fell to the ground and covered their faces. They knew this was a holy moment and a holy place.

Jesus came to them and touched them gently. "Get up," he said, "don't be afraid."

When Peter, James, and John looked up, no one was there but Jesus. The cloud was gone.

The four men started down the mountain. On the way, Jesus said, "Don't tell anyone what you saw or heard until the time is right."

The three men told no one about this transfiguration until after the resurrection of Jesus on Easter.

Prayer: God of the cloud, we heard your words, and we will listen to Jesus. Amen.

A Beautiful Garden
Genesis 2:15–17; 3:1–7

This story is from the first book of the Bible, Genesis. The stories in this part of Genesis help us understand how we are part of God's creation and how we are to live with God. Things were good with God at the beginning, but, like today, God's creatures mess up sometimes.

In this version of the story, after the LORD God created the heavens and the earth from nothing, but before the plants and animals were created, the LORD God created a human from the soil, the dirt. After all the trees, plants, and other animals were created by the LORD God, the human was placed in the garden, called Eden, to take care of it. But the fruit of one tree in the garden was off-limits to the human. This was the tree of the knowledge of good and evil. The LORD God said to the human, "You can eat all you want from every other tree and plant, but do not eat from the tree of the knowledge of good and evil. If you do, you will die."

Eden was lovely, but the human was lonely. So the LORD God created a partner to be with the human. So now there were two humans, male and female, man and woman.

Of all the animals in the garden, the snake was the smartest. The snake said to the woman, "Is it true that there is a tree in the garden that the LORD God told you not to eat its fruit?"

"We can eat all we want from any tree or plant in the whole garden, but we are not to eat from the tree in the middle of the garden," the woman answered. "If we eat fruit from it, we will die."

"Ha! You won't die," said the snake. "If you eat from that tree, you will know the difference between good and evil. You will be like the LORD God."

The woman looked at the forbidden tree. The fruit looked delicious. Wouldn't it be good to be as wise as God? So she took some fruit from the tree and gave some to the man.

As soon as they bit into the fruit, the woman and the man looked at each other and saw that they had no clothes on. They were suddenly embarrassed and sewed fig leaves together to make clothes for themselves.

I wonder what God thought about the woman and the man now.

Prayer: Creator God, like the woman and the man, we make bad choices too, but we know you are still with us. Amen.

A Night Visitor
John 3:1–17

It was night. The streets were dark, except for the moon-light. A man walked quickly to the house where Jesus was staying. The man was Nicodemus, a Pharisee, a Jewish leader who studied God's law.

"Teacher," said Nicodemus, "you are surely sent by God. I can tell from your teachings, and you have healed in ways that can be done by people only when God is with them."

Nicodemus didn't explain why, but apparently people, including the leaders, were talking about Jesus.

"Nicodemus, I can tell you," said Jesus, "unless a person has been born a new person, it is not possible to see God's kingdom."

"What are you saying, Jesus?" asked Nicodemus, puzzled at Jesus' words. "Once you are born as a baby, how can you be born again? That's impossible, isn't it?"

Jesus continued as though he hadn't heard Nicodemus at all.

"I tell you, Nicodemus, unless a person is born of water and the Spirit of God, that person cannot be part of God's kingdom. This is a different birth. Don't be puzzled that I said that you must be born a new person. God's Spirit blows wherever it wishes. You may hear its sound, but you don't know what direction it comes from or where it goes."

Nicodemus was still confused and puzzled. "How can any of what you say be true? Is this really possible?"

Jesus could probably tell from Nicodemus's voice and questions that he was confused.

Gently, Jesus answered, "Nicodemus, you are a teacher of Israel. Don't you know these things? If I tell you about things on earth and you don't understand, how can you ever understand what I tell you about the things of God that are not on earth? God loved the world so much that God sent a Son to the world, so everyone who believes in this Son will be with God forever."

Then Nicodemus left, with lots to think about.

Prayer: God of surprises, we will think about Jesus' words too. Send your Spirit to help us understand. In Jesus' name, we pray. Amen.

At a Samaritan Well
John 4:5–42

Jesus and his disciples were walking from Judea to Galilee, and the shortest route was through Samaria. Now Jews, like Jesus and the disciples, often took a longer way to avoid going through Samaria, because the Jews and the Samaritans did not get along, not at all.

At noon they stopped at the well in a Samaritan village. This well had been dug by Jacob, who had given it to his son Joseph many years ago. Jesus was tired and sat by the well to rest while the disciples went into the town to buy lunch.

A Samaritan woman came with a bucket to get water from the well. Jesus said, "Give me a drink of water."

Surprised, she said, "You, a Jewish man, are asking me, a Samaritan woman, for a drink of water?"

She knew that Jews usually avoided coming into Samaria.

"If you knew who I am," said Jesus, "you would ask *me* for a drink of water because I can give you living water."

Hands on her hips, she said, "And how would you get that water? You have no bucket, and this well is deep. Do you think you are better than Jacob, who gave us this well?"

"You drink water from this well, and you get thirsty again. If you drink my living water, you will never be thirsty."

"Well, I want some of that living water," said the woman. "Then I won't have to come here for water every day." But the woman wasn't at all sure what Jesus was talking about.

"Bring your husband here," Jesus said.

"I don't have a husband," answered the woman.

"You are right," said Jesus. "You don't have a husband now. But you have had five husbands."

This shocked the woman. How did Jesus know this about her? "You must be a prophet to know about me. I don't know many things, but I know when the Messiah from God comes, all things will be taught to us."

Quietly, Jesus said, "I am the one."

The disciples returned, and the woman left so quickly she forgot her bucket. She told her neighbors about the man at the well. They went there to see him and talk with him. Jesus taught the people in this Samaritan town for two more days before he and his disciples continued on their way to Galilee.

Prayer: Almighty God, open our minds and hearts to see Jesus as the woman at the Samaritan well did. Amen.

A Blind Man Sees
John 9:1–41

Jesus was in Jerusalem now, and each day he went to the temple to teach. On this day, Jesus and his disciples were walking along when he saw a man who was blind begging for money. The disciples asked, "Who did something wrong, the man or his parents, that he was born blind?"

"Not the man or his parents," answered Jesus. "This happened so the mighty work of God can be shown through the man."

Then Jesus spit on the ground, made mud with the spit, and rubbed it on the man's eyes. To the man, Jesus said, "Go wash in the pool of Siloam."

The man hurried away. When he came back, he could see.

His neighbors and people who used to see him begging looked at him. "Is this the blind man who used to beg here?"

Some said, "Yes," and some said, "No, they just look alike."

The man shouted, "It is me!"

"How come you can see now?" they asked.

They took the man to the Jewish leaders, who asked the man how it was that he could see. He told them, "He put

*Find a story for this week's Old Testament text, 1 Samuel 16:1–13, on page 75, "Installation of a Pastor."

mud on my eyes. I washed in the pool of Siloam and now I can see."

These Jewish leaders argued about whether the person who healed the man was from God or not. Some even thought that the man had not been born blind. So they went to his parents. "Is this your son? Was he born blind? How come he can see now?"

"Yes, he is our son. Yes, he was born blind. If you want to know how he can see now, then ask him. He is old enough to answer for himself."

For a second time, the Jewish leaders went to the man who was no longer blind. "The man you say healed you, what did he do?"

The man sighed. "I told you, and you didn't listen. Why do you want to hear it again?"

The man and the Jewish leaders argued back and forth until the leaders sent the man away. When Jesus heard this, he found the man he had healed. "Do you believe in the One sent from God?"

"Who is he?" asked the man. "I want to believe in this One."

"You have seen him," said Jesus. "He is talking to you now."

"Lord, I believe!" said the man. And he worshiped Jesus.

Prayer: Welcoming God, thank you for the stories of Jesus, especially when he shows the love you have for us. Amen.

A Vision of Bones Come Alive
Ezekiel 37:1–14

The book of Ezekiel in the Old Testament, or Hebrew Scriptures, is known for visions or dreams, with messages from God for the prophet Ezekiel. This is Ezekiel's most famous vision.

God's Spirit came over Ezekiel and took him to a big valley filled with bones. Ezekiel was plunked down right in the middle of all those bones. Then God's Spirit led Ezekiel all around this valley so he could see how many bones were there and that they were old and dry. A valley filled with dry bones!

"Human," said God, "can these bones come alive again?"

Ezekiel knew the answer, "Only you, the LORD God, can answer that question."

As if to prove that Ezekiel was right, God told him to say to the bones, "Listen, bones! The LORD God says to you, 'I am going to breathe life into you. You will be alive again! I will put muscles on you. I will cover the muscles with flesh and skin. Then I will breathe life into you. When you come alive, you will know that I am God.'"

Ezekiel did exactly as God told him, using the very same words. When he stopped talking, a great rattling and a tremendous shaking began. The bones came together to form skeletons. Then the skeletons were covered with muscle and the muscles were covered with flesh and skin. But these bodies just lay on the ground, for they were not yet alive.

Again God spoke to Ezekiel. "Speak to the breath and say, 'The LORD God says to you, "Come from the four winds. Breathe life into these dead bodies."'"

Again Ezekiel did exactly as God told him, using the very same words. In the blink of an eye, the bodies came alive and stood up. Ezekiel was surrounded by a great crowd of people, maybe more than he could count.

Ezekiel was speechless. He didn't know what to think. Then God explained the vision to him. "These bones are the people of Israel. While they are forced to live in Babylon, away from home, they feel dead and have no hope. They are sure they are finished. I want you to tell the people these words from me: I am giving breath and life to you. I will take you to a good land where you can plant and grow food. Then you will know that I am God. This is what the Lord says."

Can you imagine how the people forced to live in Babylon felt when they heard this message from God?

Prayer: God, who brings life, when we forget that you are God, remind us of the valley of dry bones vision so we remember that you bring life and hope. Amen.

Hosanna!
Matthew 21:1–11

It had been a long journey, but Jesus and his disciples were almost to Jerusalem. When they arrived in Bethphage on the Mount of Olives, Jesus led his friends to a place where they could see the tall city wall of Jerusalem.

But they weren't going to walk quietly into the city with other Jews heading there to celebrate the Passover. No, Jesus had another plan in mind.

He motioned for two of his disciples to come to him: "Go into that village. Right away, you will see a donkey and a colt tied up. Bring them to me. If someone questions you, say that the Lord needs them."

The two disciples did exactly what Jesus said. When they got to the village, they found the donkey and the colt. When someone asked what they were doing, they said, "The Lord needs them."

They led the donkey and the colt back to where Jesus was waiting. The disciples laid their clothes on the backs of the animals. Jesus sat on the donkey, and the group headed for Jerusalem.

Along the way, people watched Jesus riding on the donkey. Some spread their clothes on the road for the donkey to walk on. Others cut branches from the palm trees and laid them on the road. It was like a parade! Crowds of people gathered to see what was happening.

Some people shouted, "Hosanna to the Son of David! Blessings on the one who comes in the name of the Lord! Hosanna in the highest!"

More people began to shout until it seemed like everyone was shouting, "Hosanna!"

"Who is this man?" people asked.

"He is the prophet Jesus of Nazareth in Galilee," was the answer.

Prayer: Lord God, today we join the crowd in shouting praises to Jesus, your Son. Amen.

Surprised by Jesus
Matthew 28:1–10

Night was almost over and Sabbath was ending. It was nearly light enough to see where you were walking. But Mary of Magdala and Mary the mother of Jesus' disciples James and John were up and ready to leave the house. They picked up the jars of herbs and spices to put over the body of Jesus. On Friday, they had sadly followed Joseph of Arimathea as he had Jesus' body placed in a tomb. They knew exactly where to go now.

They walked quietly. No words could say how sad they were. Even the birds seemed quiet this morning.

When they got to the tomb, an earthquake shook the ground under their feet. At the same time, an angel, a messenger from God, stood in front of them. His clothes were so white they could hardly look in his direction. They watched as the angel rolled the heavy stone from the opening of the tomb.

The Jewish leaders, afraid the disciples would come for Jesus' body, had stationed temple guards at the tomb. These strong guards were shaking and so frightened that they could not move.

The angel turned to the women and said, "Don't be afraid.

You are looking for Jesus in the tomb. Jesus isn't here. He is no longer dead. Jesus is alive! Remember, he told you this would happen. Come, see where his body was. Now go tell Jesus' disciples what you have seen here and that they are to meet him in Galilee."

So excited, the two women, Mary of Magdala and Mary the mother of James and John, ran back to find the disciples and tell them the message. But before they got there, Jesus stood in front of them. The two women fell to their knees and worshiped him. "It's all right," said Jesus. "Go tell my friends to go to Galilee. I will see them there."

Prayer: God of Glory, we are so happy to be here on this special day. Thank you for the gift of Jesus, who shows us how you love us and how to show that love to others. In Jesus' name, we pray. Amen.

A Surprise Visit
John 20:19–31

The first surprise on that Easter morning was when the women found an empty tomb. But that wasn't the only surprise that day.

That evening, all the disciples—well, all except Thomas—were in a building with the doors locked. Now that the guards had reported that Jesus' body was missing from the tomb, the disciples were afraid they were going to be in big trouble. Here they were, excited that the women had seen Jesus and terrified of the Jewish leaders and what they might do, happy and scared all at the same time.

They were chatting quietly among themselves when Jesus stood in the middle of the room. What? No one had opened the door, but here was Jesus! He said, "Peace be with you."

Jesus showed the disciples the wounds on his hands and his side. When they saw that this was really Jesus, they were wild with happiness. Their chatter was not quiet now, but bubbling over.

Again, Jesus said to them, "Peace be with you. Just as my Father, God, sent me, I send you."

Then Jesus breathed on them, each one of them, and said, "Receive the Holy Spirit. If you forgive a person, that person is forgiven. If you don't forgive a person, that person is not forgiven."

Later, when Jesus was gone, Thomas returned. They all spoke at once, saying, "We have seen Jesus."

"Well, I won't believe you until I see the wounds on his hands and side for myself," said Thomas.

Eight days later, the disciples—Thomas too—were in the same room as before, and even though the doors were locked, Jesus stood in the middle of them. As before, he said, "Peace be with you."

He walked over to Thomas and said, "See the wounds on my hands. Touch the wound in my side. Now you can believe."

Thomas gasped, "My Lord and my God!"

"You believe because you see me. How happy will be the people who do not see me and still believe," said Jesus.

Prayer: God of Glory, the continuing story of that first Easter does make us happy, even though we cannot see Jesus. Amen.

❧ THIRD SUNDAY OF EASTER ❦

Another Easter Day Surprise
Luke 24:13–35

It was the same day that the women found the empty tomb.
And it was the same day that Jesus stood among the disciples in the locked room and said "Peace be with you." And, on that same day, two other followers of Jesus were on the road to the town of Emmaus. Now that Jesus was gone, they decided they might as well go home.

Cleopas and another disciple, perhaps his wife, talked as they walked. They remembered how it was to listen to Jesus tell stories about the kingdom of God. They smiled as they remembered the people Jesus had healed. They grew sad as they remembered the past week when Jesus was arrested and then died. They were so busy remembering that they didn't notice that someone was walking beside them.

"What are you talking about?" asked the man.

Cleopas said, "Are you the only person coming from Jerusalem who doesn't know what happened there?"

"What happened?" he asked.

"Jesus of Nazareth, a prophet of God, was arrested and put to death on a cross. We thought he would save Israel. Now we don't know. Earlier today, women from our group went to the tomb, and it was empty. A messenger from God said he is alive, but we didn't see Jesus."

"Have you forgotten what the prophets said about the one God would send?" asked the man. "Wake up! Wasn't this all to happen?" He went on to teach them about the prophets, beginning with Moses.

When they got to Emmaus, the two disciples said, "It's getting dark. Stay with us for the night."

So the man came in with them. When the food was on the table, the man took the bread, blessed it, and broke it. He gave some to each person. Suddenly, in that moment, the two followers of Jesus knew deep inside that this man was Jesus. Then, just as suddenly, he was gone.

They looked at each other. "Wasn't his teaching powerful?"

They left immediately to go back to Jerusalem to find the disciples so they could tell them what had happened. When they got there, the disciples were excited too because Peter had also seen Jesus. What an Easter day that was!

Prayer: God of Glory, the excitement of that first Easter day, from morning until night, fills us with joy and happiness. Thanks be to you. Amen.

The New Community
Acts 2:42–47

Now Peter and the other apostles were without Jesus, but they had not forgotten Jesus and all he taught them. Peter told a crowd of people about Jesus in Jerusalem on the day of the Jewish festival of Pentecost, and many people joined the apostles as believers. Some of these people stayed in Jerusalem to learn more about Jesus.

But they didn't only listen to the disciples' stories about Jesus. They helped one another. They ate their meals together. They prayed together.

The more they did together, the closer they felt to God and Jesus. The apostles did many wonders and healings.

During these days, the new believers were one community. They sold their land and other possessions and gave the money to anyone of the group who needed something.

Every day, they went to the temple to pray and praise God just as they had done before. They prayed together, and they prayed alone. They knew prayer was a way to be close to God and to remember Jesus.

They gathered in their homes and ate meals together. With great joy, they put all their food together and ate. Everyone who saw them being one community noticed how they loved God and showed God's goodness to everyone.

During these days, new people joined them every day through the grace of God.

Prayer: God of grace, we learn from this story of the first believers in Jesus how we can live as one community, the church, too. In Jesus' name, we pray. Amen.

A Strong Faith
Acts 7:55–60

When Jesus left and put Peter and the other apostles in charge, they had a lot of work to do. They taught the new believers. They made sure everyone got food. Big jobs and little jobs. With so many people now learning together, praying together, eating together, it isn't surprising that a problem appeared. One group thought its widows, women whose husbands had died, weren't getting their fair share of food. They complained to the apostles.

It was clear to Peter and the other apostles that they didn't have time to take care of all these problems. They needed help. When Jesus knew there was more teaching and healing than he could do, he called disciples to help him. Now the apostles chose seven men to be deacons. These deacons would make sure that everyone got enough food. One of the men chosen was Stephen. He was respected for his strong faith and the good works he did.

Of course, these deacons still went to the temple to pray every day. One day when Stephen went to the temple, things did not go well. He got into an argument with some Jews who did not believe that Jesus was the Son of God. These Jews weren't winning the argument so they got some other Jews to lie about Stephen so they could get him into trouble with the Jewish high priest.

They took Stephen to the high priest. The men who had agreed to lie about Stephen said that Stephen said Jesus would destroy the temple and change the laws God gave to Moses. The high priest was shocked.

"Are these men telling the truth?" he asked Stephen.

"These men, all of you, are stubborn. You are no better than people who don't believe in God," shouted Stephen.

Not a good answer for the high priest. The high priest, the council, and all the other Jews present were angry, really angry. They dragged Stephen out of the city to be stoned to death.

According to Jewish law, the first people to throw stones were those who had accused Stephen. These men placed their coats at the feet of Saul. Then they began throwing stones at Stephen.

As the stones peppered down on Stephen, he prayed, "Lord Jesus, take me, but forgive them for doing this to me." And then he died.

Prayer: God of power and might, we pray that our faith in you and Jesus will grow as strong as the faith of Stephen. Amen.

Never Alone

John 14:15–21

One of the stories Peter and the apostles taught new believers was something that Jesus said when they celebrated the Passover in Jerusalem just before Jesus died.

On that evening, the day we call Maundy Thursday, Jesus and his closest friends gathered in a room just outside Jerusalem. Jesus knew that he would soon be leaving his friends. For three years, they had traveled together all over Judea and Galilee. They were very good friends.

That night as they sat around the Passover table, Jesus said:

"I have some rules for you to follow when I am no longer with you. If you love me, you will keep these commandments. But you will not be alone. I will ask my Father to send you another friend, a companion, the Holy Spirit, to be with you forever. Only you, my friends, will know this companion. Other people will not know this special friend. This friend will live in you and always be with you.

"I won't leave you all alone. I will be with you. I will live in you. When you keep my commandments, you show that you love me. If you love me, you know that my Father loves you."

Jesus' friends, the apostles, didn't know what to make of these words. Why would Jesus leave them? But the good news was that Jesus would not leave them alone. Jesus wants us to know that too.

Prayer: Loving God, we are happy to know that Jesus will always be with us and that you are with us too. Amen.

Time to Say Good-bye
Acts 1:6–14

Six weeks had gone by since Jesus had appeared to the disciples, Jesus' followers, in the locked room in Jerusalem. They had enjoyed many times with Jesus in those weeks, but Jesus knew that it was time to say good-bye.

On that day, Jesus told his friends that he had something important to say to them.

Everyone was listening carefully when Jesus said, "Wait in Jerusalem for the Holy Spirit to come to you. The Spirit will fill you with power. Then you will be able to tell my story, the story of God's great love in Jerusalem, in Judea, and in Samaria. But you won't stop there."

What does Jesus mean? wondered the disciples.

As the disciples were thinking about Jesus' words, Jesus was taken up into a cloud and disappeared. As they were staring at the cloud, two men dressed in white robes said to them, "Why are you staring at the sky? Jesus will come again the same way he left."

Then all the disciples went back to Jerusalem. They went back to the room where they had often seen Jesus, to wait for the Holy Spirit. As they waited, they along with some women, including Mary the mother of Jesus, and Jesus' brothers spent their time praying and praising God.

I wonder how long they will have to wait before the Holy Spirit comes to them.

Prayer: Holy God, we wait with the followers of Jesus so long ago for the gift of your Holy Spirit. Amen.

A Gift from God
Acts 2:1–21

Jesus was gone. Now all the followers of Jesus could do was wait. So they went back to Jerusalem. The city was crowded with Jews from many countries who had come to celebrate the festival of Pentecost. If you stood in one spot, you might hear sixteen different languages. Yet everyone had come to Jerusalem to bring offerings of grain to the temple.

Day after day, Jesus' followers waited. On this day, when they were all together in one room, suddenly, a sound like a mighty rushing wind blew through the room. It filled each corner and nook. The disciples looked around. What was happening?

At the same time, what looked like little flames of fire danced over their heads. What was this? The wind didn't put out the flames and the flames didn't burn anyone. What was happening?

Then, the wind stopped and the flames disappeared and the Holy Spirit came, dancing and powerful. It moved from person to person, filling each one. Next the people were able to speak in languages they had never known before.

All this noise and commotion attracted a crowd on the

street outside. When the people listened carefully, they could hear their own languages spoken inside the room.

"What is this?" they asked one another. "How can these people who are not from our countries speak our languages? They must be drunk."

Peter answered them. "We are not drunk on wine. It is only nine o'clock in the morning. We have been filled with God's Holy Spirit as was promised long ago by the prophets."

He told the crowd all about Jesus and the message that God's love was for everyone. The Holy Spirit blew through the crowd and many people believed what Peter said about Jesus, and they joined the disciples that day.

When the people who had been filled with the Holy Spirit returned to their countries, they told their families and neighbors about Jesus. The message of Jesus spread across the lands. Now, many, many years later, that message comes to us today, just as the Holy Spirit comes to us, too.

Prayer: God of the Spirit, send your Spirit to us this day so we may be filled with eagerness to tell the world about Jesus. Amen.

God's Work
Genesis 1:1–4a

Imagine nothing but darkness, emptiness, nothingness. Now imagine God breathing, blowing wind over this emptiness so that light shines in some of the darkness. God says, "This is good!" Evening comes, and then morning: the first day.

Then God separates the waters below from the sky above. God says, "This is good!" Evening comes, and then morning: the second day.

God pushes the waters together so dry land can be seen. On that dry land, plants and trees grow. God says, "This is good!" Evening comes, and then morning: the third day.

Now God has a space, a world. But God needs something that will tell day from night and when the seasons change. So God puts stars and the moon in the sky at night and the sun in the day. Now there are day and night, months and years. God says, "This is good!" Evening comes, and then morning: the fourth day.

The space, the world, is ready for living creatures. First come creatures who live in the waters: frogs, fish, fiddler crabs, maybe a frisky sea lion pup. Then come the creatures that fly in the sky: birds, bumblebees, butterflies, maybe bats.

God says, "This is good!" and God blesses them and tells them to fill the waters and the sky. Evening comes, and then morning: the fifth day.

Now it is time for the creatures that live on the dry land: cows, cats, crawling bugs, and then human beings, you and me, human beings made in God's image. God blesses them all, but to the human beings, God says, "Take care of all creation. The plants and the fruit from the trees are for you to eat. I give the grasses to the other living creatures to eat." God looks around at all that God has made and says, "This is really, really good!" Evening comes, and then morning: the sixth day.

On the seventh day, everything in this space, this world, is already created. God has nothing else to do. So God rests on the seventh day and makes it a holy day, a special day to rest from all work. Yes, God rests on the seventh day.

Prayer: Creator God, with your breath, your wind, you created all that we see and have, including us. We praise you! Amen.

*(Sunday between May 24 and May 28 inclusive,
if after Trinity Sunday)*

Wait for God
Psalm 131

If you open a Bible to about the middle, you will probably open to the book of Psalms in the Old Testament, or
Hebrew Scriptures. Psalms has more chapters than any other
book of the Bible: one hundred and fifty. If you turn to Psalm
120, you will see that it is called a pilgrimage song, or in some
Bibles, a song of ascent. Fifteen psalms are titled this way
because they were probably sung or prayed as people walked
up to Jerusalem to go to the temple.

Some of these psalms of ascent or going up are famous.
We hear parts of them in hymns we sing or they are part of
the Call to Worship. "I lift up my eyes to the hills— / from
where will my help come?" (Psalm 121). Or "I was glad
when they said to me, / 'Let us go to the house of the LORD!'"
(Psalm 122).

These psalms remind the people about God and how God
is with us. Today's psalm is 131. Imagine that you are walking to Jerusalem. The road is rocky and uneven, but you can
finally see the huge city wall surrounding Jerusalem. As you
walk, you say to yourself:

> "God, my heart is not proud.
>   I do not look up as though I am better than others.

"I don't try to do things
  that are too great or beyond me.
"No, my whole being is quiet and calm,
    as relaxed and content as a child being hugged
      by its mother.
"People of God, wait for God.
    now and forever."

Imagine how calm these words would make you feel, even though you are excited to be so near to Jerusalem.

Prayer: Comforting God, we are so happy that we can remember these words from Psalm 131 and know that you will calm us too. Amen.

(Sunday between May 29 and June 4 inclusive)

SEMICONTINUOUS

A Great Flood
Genesis 6:9–22, 7:24, 8:14–19*

This story is about a man named Noah and how he obeyed God. It is found in the book of Genesis, the first book of the Old Testament, or Hebrew Scriptures. The stories in the early chapters of Genesis were told to help people understand who God is. This is the story of Noah and the great flood.

Things were not going well with God's creation. Everyone—everyone, that is, but Noah and his family—had forgotten about God. God said to Noah, "Build a wooden ark, a big ship." Then God told Noah exactly what size to make this ark and exactly how it should look. "Noah," said God, "Go into the ark. Take your wife and your sons and their wives. Take a pair, a male and a female, of every living creature onto the ark. Oh, yes, and take food for you and all the living creatures."

Noah did just what God said. It was a little tricky to get a pair of each living creature, but Noah managed. When they were all in the ark, it began to rain. It rained for one hundred

---

*At this point the lectionary offers two streams: the semicontinuous one and the complementary one. The Old Testament stories for most of the Sundays for the rest of the church year are from the semicontinuous stream. For those Sundays, an additional story from the complementary stream or the common New Testament text is provided.

fifty days. The land was covered with water, but Noah, his family, and all those pairs of living creatures were safely in the ark.

Seven months after the rain stopped, Noah could see just the top of Mount Ararat. Ten months after the rain stopped, more mountaintops peeked above the water. Forty days after that, Noah opened the window of the ark and let a raven, a big black bird, out, and it flew back and forth over the water until it found dry land. Then Noah set loose a dove, a lovely grey bird, to look for a dry place to land. But it came back and Noah took it into the ark. Seven days later, Noah set the dove loose again. When it returned this time, it had the leaf from an olive tree in its beak. Noah waited seven more days and sent the dove out again. This time the dove did not come back. Noah knew that the water had gone down and the dove had found a place to build its nest.

Finally, God said to Noah, "You and your family should leave the ark. Take all of the living creatures out of the ark too, so they can live on the earth." The flood was over and Noah's family would start a new home on the earth.

Prayer: God, you saved Noah and his family and the living creatures that you created. We put our hope in you. Amen.

Remember and Obey
Deuteronomy 11:18–21, 26–28

Moses and the Israelite people had walked through the desert wilderness for forty years. Even though God was with them, it was hard. Now they were almost to the land God had promised them.

God gave Moses the Ten Commandments on two slabs of rock. These important words helped the people remember that they were God's people and how to live in God's ways.

Now the Israelites were about to begin a new life, and God had more words for them, words about remembering. Moses called the people together and said:

"Keep the words from God, especially the Ten Commandments, in your heart. Know them so well that they are deep within you. Tie them in a box on your hand. Tie them in a box to your forehead so you won't forget them."

People nodded. Yes, they could do that. Moses continued:

"Teach them to your children when they get up in the morning and when they go to bed at night. Talk about them when you are in your house and when you are traveling."

That sounded like a bit more work, but the people thought they could do it.

Moses had more to say:

"Write them on the side of your doors so you will remember them every time you leave and every time you return. Do this remembering and obeying God's words and you will live long in your new homeland and you will be blessed by God."

Moses paused to let all these words sink into the people. Then he said, "Pay attention! You have a choice. You can do these things and be right with God, but if you don't do them, you will find yourself going away from God."

The people chose to live in God's ways, but that wasn't so easy either.

Prayer: God of Moses and the Israelites and our God too, we want to remember you and obey you. Amen.

❧ PROPER 5 ❧
(Sunday between June 5 and June 11 inclusive)

A Woman and a Girl Healed
Matthew 9:9–13, 18–26*

Jesus was talking to some people when a man dressed in rich clothes ran to him and dropped to his knees at Jesus' feet. Everyone was surprised. The man said, "Help! My daughter has died. I know that if you come and place your hands on her she will live."

Jesus stopped what he was doing and he and the disciples left with the man.

On the way, a woman who had been sick for twelve years came near Jesus, close behind him. She touched his clothes, for she thought if she could just touch Jesus she would get better.

Jesus turned and saw her. "Woman, cheer up! Your faith has made you better." That woman, who had been sick for twelve years, wasn't sick any more.

When Jesus and the disciples got to the house of the man whose daughter had died, all the people there were crying. Jesus said to them, "Go away! The little girl isn't dead. She's just asleep."

---

*This lectionary text includes the call of Matthew, which will be part of the introduction in the story for Proper 6.

The people at the house laughed at Jesus. Then he sent all the people away and Jesus went to the room where the little girl was and gently touched her hand. At Jesus' touch, the little girl got up.

This was big news and it was told from house to house and village to village all over the land.

Prayer: Healing God, thank you for the doctors, nurses, and other health care workers who take care of us today. In Jesus' name, we pray. Amen.

❧ PROPER 6 ❧
(Sunday between June 12 and June 18 inclusive)

Sending the Twelve
Matthew 9:35–10:8 (9–23)

From the time after his baptism, Jesus gathered disciples who would travel with him wherever he went. The first disciples he chose were fishing in the Sea of Galilee. Two sets of brothers—Simon Peter and Andrew, and James and John—left their fishing boats and nets to travel with Jesus.

One day Jesus saw a tax collector named Matthew sitting at his table collecting taxes. Now the Jews did not like tax collectors, not at all. Tax collectors worked for the hated Roman government. Many of them were dishonest and collected more taxes than they were supposed to collect. People didn't talk to or invite tax collectors to their homes. But Jesus, even though he knew no one liked them, stopped and talked to Matthew. "Follow me," said Jesus.

Matthew did. That evening Jesus went to Matthew's house and had dinner with Matthew and other tax collectors. Now the Pharisees, important Jewish leaders, saw this and asked Jesus' disciples, "Why does your master eat with tax collectors?"

Jesus heard them and answered, "I didn't come to hang around good people but to help those whom no one else will help."

By now Jesus had twelve disciples who were always with him. He said to them, "You have the power to heal every sickness. It will soon be time for you to go out into the villages without me to do what I do."

But Jesus had more instructions for the twelve disciples before they would go out on their own. He said, "Go only to the people of Israel. Announce, 'The kingdom of heaven is near.' Heal people who are sick and who have skin diseases. Don't accept money for what you do. Don't take anything extra, like a bag with clothes. If you find someone good in a place, stay with that family. When you enter a house, say, 'Peace.' If people are mean to you, leave that place right away and don't go back. Don't worry about what to say because God's Spirit will give you words."

That is only part of the instructions Jesus told the twelve disciples. It was a lot to remember.

Prayer: God of love, we know that you want the church today to follow Jesus' instructions too. Give us courage. Amen.

Jeremiah Complains
Jeremiah 20:7–13

Jeremiah didn't want to be a prophet for God, but God insisted. It didn't go well with Jeremiah as a prophet of God. The job of a prophet was to give messages from God to God's people, and mostly, God's people didn't want to hear them.

When Jeremiah tried to talk to the people, they didn't listen. Jeremiah warned them over and over that if they didn't listen, trouble would come, and the people laughed. The leaders sent people to beat him up and put him in prison. One time they pushed Jeremiah into a well. Being God's prophet was no fun!

Jeremiah was lonely. People made fun of him. No matter what he did they didn't listen to God's message. He had had enough, so he cried out to God in a prayer that is in our Bible. Jeremiah prayed:

> "God, you tricked me.
> "I gave your people the message,
>   but they laughed at me.
> "They make fun of me day after day.

"Sometimes I don't even want to think of you, God.
   I don't want to say your name.
"Then your words burn inside my heart and I have
         to say them.
   Even then, the crowds whisper and make fun
         of me.
"They are just waiting for me to make a mistake.
"But, God, you are like a strong soldier standing
         next to me.
"I have complained to you.
   Now I will wait to see what you do.
"I sing praises to you, God.
   I know you rescue those who have been hurt by
         their enemies."

As angry as Jeremiah was, he still knew that God was with him and understood how he felt.

Prayer: Strong God, from Jeremiah we learn that you listen to all our prayers, even when we are angry. Amen.

Rules for the Road
*Matthew 10:24–39**

Shortly after Jesus began to teach about God and to heal people, he invited two sets of brothers to be his disciples. They were James and John, sons of Zebedee, and Peter, also known as Simon Peter, and Andrew. But he needed more followers than these four. In the weeks that followed he called eight more to be his disciples: Philip, Bartholomew, Thomas, Matthew, James, Thaddaeus, Simon, and Judas. We call them the Twelve Disciples, or simply the Twelve.

Now he wanted them to go to villages on their own and teach about God and heal people as he did. He gathered them together and gave them the power to do this. Then he told them, "Tell people that God's plan for creation is near. Heal people who are sick. Do not ask people to pay you, for you received this power without paying for it. Don't take any extra clothes; travel lightly. Leave a town if the people are not friendly to you."

Good things to remember, thought the disciples. But Jesus had more to say, "What I am telling you, shout boldly from

---

*This story begins with the opening of Matthew 10 and gives some background to the lectionary passage.

the rooftops. Don't be afraid. God knows what is happening to each bird that flies in the sky, so you know that God will be with you."

Jesus taught the Twelve Disciples much more. When he finished, all of them—Simon Peter, Andrew, James, John, Philip, Bartholomew, Thomas, Matthew, James, Thaddaeus, Simon, and Judas—set out to tell people about God's plan for all creation and to heal people who were sick.

Prayer: Amazing God, you sent Jesus to teach us about you. May we teach others about you too. In Jesus' name we pray. Amen.

(Sunday between June 26 and July 2 inclusive)

How to Welcome Others
Matthew 10:40–42

Every day Jesus taught the disciples something new that they would need to know to follow him. They were eager to listen to him as he talked about God's love and God's ways. Jesus wanted to prepare these good friends for the time when they would go to towns and villages on their own, a time when he was no longer with them.

"Good friends," Jesus began, "the day will come when you will go from town to town to teach the people about God's love and God's ways as I do now. Some people will be happy to hear your words. These people will welcome you with joy. But other people will not be happy to hear you. Do not be upset. That is to be expected. But remember, anyone who welcomes you also welcomes me, for you go in my name. Anyone who welcomes me also welcomes God.

The disciples knew what he was saying. The crowds who came to hear Jesus were large; but the disciples knew that not everyone who came liked what Jesus said.

Jesus went on, "Sometimes you will welcome others. When you welcome them, you also welcome me. And when you welcome me, you also welcome God."

Someone said, "Yes, we can do that."

Just to be sure they got what he was saying, Jesus continued, "The smallest things can make a person feel welcome. When someone is thirsty, especially after walking all day, giving that person a drink of water is the best welcome of all. When you or anyone does this kind of thing, you are showing God's love."

Aha, the disciples thought, *when we show love to others, we are showing God's love. When we welcome others, we are welcoming God.*

The disciples remembered Jesus' words when Jesus was not with them. After many years, someone wrote them down so they would never be forgotten. Today, when we welcome others, we welcome Jesus and God. When we do loving things for others, we show our love for Jesus and for God.

Prayer: Welcoming God, prepare our hearts so we can show your love and welcome to every one we meet. In Jesus' name, we pray. Amen.

A Wife for Isaac
Genesis 24:34–38, 42–49, 58–67

When Abraham and Sarah were very old, they had a baby boy and named him Isaac. When he was grown up, it was time for Isaac to marry a wife. So Abraham called for his oldest and most faithful servant and said, "Go back to my land Haran and find a wife for Isaac. I will give you ten camels to carry all you will need and gifts for the bride and her family."

The servant left for Haran. When he stopped to water the camels in Haran, he asked God for a sign so he would know which woman was the right one for Isaac. Before long a beautiful young woman came to get water from the spring. The servant asked for a sip of water from her jug. "Drink," she said. "Then I will get water for your camels."

This was the sign. This young woman had done something good for the servant. The servant gave her a gold ring and two gold bracelets. Then he asked, "Does your father have room for me to spend the night and bed down my camels?"

"Yes," she answered, "we have plenty of straw and feed for your camels. There is also a place for you to spend the night."

The young woman, who was named Rebekah, hurried home to tell her family what had happened at the spring. Her brother Laban left to find the man to urge him to stay with them. When they got to the family's tents, the servant went inside and Laban took care of the ten camels.

Before he would eat, the servant said to Rebekah's father and brother, "I am a servant of Abraham, who is a rich man. Abraham and Sarah have a son Isaac. They sent me here to find a wife for him. When your daughter gave me water to drink and even offered to water my camels, I knew God had given me a sign. Tell me if I shall take her back with me."

They called to Rebekah and asked her, "Will you go with this man to be the wife of Isaac?"

"I will go," she said. She and her servants left with Abraham's servant immediately.

Each day they were closer to where Abraham's tents were pitched. One evening, when Isaac was checking the fields, he saw camels in the distance. Rebekah saw Isaac and got down from her camel. "Who is this man coming toward us?" she asked Abraham's servant.

"It is my master," said the servant. When she heard this Rebekah took off her headdress and covered herself. The servant told Isaac how he had found Rebekah and Isaac took Rebekah to his mother Sarah's tent. Isaac married Rebekah and loved her.

Prayer: God of Abraham, Sarah, Isaac, and Rebekah, these people followed you faithfully. We will try to follow you faithfully too. Amen.

(Sunday between July 3 and July 9 inclusive)

GOSPEL

Rest for the Tired
Matthew 11:28–30

As Jesus traveled from town to town, he saw how many people wanted to hear his message about God's love, and some always wanted to be healed. He couldn't do all this by himself, so he chose twelve disciples to be his special friends and helpers. We call them the Disciples (with a capital *D*), the Twelve (with a capital *T*), or the Twelve Disciples.

Jesus spent quite a while teaching the Twelve Disciples so they could teach and heal just as he did. When he finished, he walked again to the towns and villages to teach and heal there. When he came to cities where he had been and they weren't doing what he had taught them, he scolded the people. He was not happy with them.

In other places, he looked at the crowd of people gathered around him. Some had brought sick people to be healed. Others wanted to hear more about God. Some looked tired and worn out. To those people Jesus said,

"Come to me if you are struggling to live each day. Come to me if you are loaded down with worries. Come to me if you have too much to do. Come to me and I will give you rest. Learn from me how to live even when life is hard. Learn how to be gentle and loving. I will help you with your troubles. Then you will find rest too."

I wonder what these people said to each other or to their neighbors when they got home.

Prayer: God of the tired and weary, may we keep Jesus' words in our hearts, so when we are tired and weary, we will remember to turn to him. In Jesus' name, we pray. Amen.

(Sunday between July 10 and July 16 inclusive)

SEMICONTINUOUS

Twins for Isaac and Rebekah
Genesis 25:19–34

Isaac, the son of Abraham and Sarah, married Rebekah, the woman Abraham's servant had brought back from Haran. They were eager to have children. Isaac prayed to God that Rebekah would have a baby. God heard Isaac's prayer, and soon Rebekah was pregnant.

During this time, Rebekah prayed to God whenever she didn't feel well, which was often. God told her, "The babies in you stand for two countries, two different peoples. One will be stronger than the other. The older baby will be a servant of the younger one."

Yes, Rebekah was having twins. The first baby was born: a boy, red all over and lots of hair on his body. Rebekah named this baby Esau. The second baby was born, holding to the heel of baby Esau. Rebekah called this baby boy Jacob.

The two boys grew up and were very different. Esau liked to go outdoors and hunt for animals, but Jacob would rather stay at home. Their father Isaac liked Esau because Isaac liked to eat the animals that Esau hunted. But Rebekah liked Jacob best.

One day, Jacob was cooking stew. Esau had been out hunting. When he came in, he smelled that stew. Oh my, was he hungry. "Let me have some of that good smelling stew," he said to Jacob.

"Give me the rights you have as the oldest son," said Jacob. He saw that this was his big chance to get something from his brother.

"Well, I'll die someday anyway, what good are my rights as the oldest son?" muttered Esau.

"Give me your word right now," urged Jacob.

Oh, did that stew smell yummy! Esau's mouth was watering. "Okay," he said, and agreed to give Jacob the rights Esau had as the oldest son. And Esau immediately ate the stew and bread, thinking no more about his rights as the oldest son . . . that he didn't have anymore.

This could only lead to trouble for someone; you will hear more about these brothers.

Prayer: God, sometimes we try to trick people like Jacob did, and sometimes we don't think things through like Esau. Help us keep our thinking straight so we follow your ways. Amen.

❧ PROPER 10 ❧
(Sunday between July 10 and 16 inclusive)

GOSPEL

Seeds and Good Soil
Matthew 13:1–9, 18–23

On this day, Jesus was sitting by the lake. A lot of people gathered around him, so he climbed into a boat that was nearby. He sat in the boat and told the crowd this story:

"A farmer went out to plant seeds in his field. He had a bag of seeds and he scattered them by throwing them as he walked. (*Demonstrate flinging seeds to the side.*) Some seeds fell on the path by the field. That ground was hard, and birds quickly came to eat those seeds.

"Other seeds fell on ground that was filled with little and big rocks, and there wasn't much soil. When these seeds grew and the sun came out, their roots weren't deep enough to get nourishment, and the sun dried them up.

"Some more seeds fell among the thorny plants. These thick thorny plants grew faster than the seeds did, and the seeds couldn't grow.

"But some seeds fell on good soil, where they got just the right sunshine and water, and no other plants were there to crowd them. These seeds grew into strong plants and gave the farmer more than was expected. If you have ears, pay attention to this story."

Prayer: Loving God, may we listen carefully to Jesus' story of the farmer and the seeds so that we hear your word to us in Jesus' story. In Jesus' name, we pray. Amen.

(Sunday between July 17 and 23 inclusive)

SEMICONTINUOUS

An Escape and a Dream
Genesis 28:10–19a

Jacob tricked his twin brother Esau again, and now Esau was angry, angry enough to kill Jacob.

Their mother, Rebekah, was worried. "Jacob, you must leave," she said. "Today, start for your uncle's land. Stay there until Esau calms down. I will let you know when it is safe for you to come back here."

Jacob immediately tied his things to a camel and set off for his uncle's. When the sun began to set, and it was time to stop after the first day, Jacob spread a blanket on the ground and used a rock for a pillow. He was really tired, so he fell asleep right away.

During the night, Jacob dreamed a very unusual dream. He dreamed that he saw a staircase that went from the ground all the way up through the clouds, so he couldn't see where it ended. But that wasn't all. Angels walked up and down the stairs.

In the dream, as he watched the angels walking up and down the stairs, God stood beside him and said, "I am the God of your grandparents, Abraham and Sarah, and of your parents, Isaac and Rebekah."

Then, to Jacob, who had tricked his brother and lied to

his father, God said, "I am always with you. I will look after you wherever you go. One day I will bring you back to your home. You will be the father of many generations and because of you every family on earth will be blessed. I am your God, and I make this promise to you."

When Jacob woke up, he looked around. "God is in this place, and I didn't know it when I stopped here. This is a place to see God."

Jacob stood up. He took the stone he had used for a pillow and marked this spot as a holy place that he called *Bethel*, which means "God's house." Then Jacob put his blanket on the camel and continued his journey to his uncle's land. God was with him day and night.

Prayer: God, you are with us just as you were with Jacob, day and night, even when we do something wrong. We praise you for this. Amen.

GOSPEL

Seeds and Weeds
Matthew 13:24–30, 36–43

On the same day that Jesus sat in the boat and told the story of the farmer planting seeds, he told the crowd of people this story, also about a farmer:

"The kingdom of heaven, God's plan for all creation, is like a farmer who planted good seeds to grow wheat in the field. While the farmer and the workers were sleeping, someone who did not like the farmer planted weeds in the same field and sneaked away.

"When the seeds, both the wheat and the weeds, began to grow roots and show little sprouts above the ground, the workers could see that there were weeds all over the field, growing next to the wheat.

"They hurried to the farmer and said, 'Didn't you plant good seeds in the field? Why are there so many weeds?'

'Someone who doesn't like me has planted those weeds,' said the farmer.

'Should we pull up the weeds?' they asked.

'No,' said the farmer, 'If you pull them up, you'll pull up the wheat plants too. Let them both grow until it is time to cut the wheat. Then I will tell the harvest workers to gather the weeds and burn them. But the wheat will be put in my barn.'"

Prayer: Creator God, Jesus' stories teach many things. Help us to listen and think about them carefully. In Jesus' name, we pray. Amen.

(Sunday between July 24 and July 30 inclusive)

The House Church in Rome
Romans 8:26–39

After that special Pentecost Day when the Holy Spirit came to the disciples who were waiting in Jerusalem, the good news about Jesus and God's love spread to lands far away. Some of the believers in Jesus lived in the city of Rome, many miles across the sea from Jerusalem.

They gathered in someone's home, because this was before church buildings were built. It was called a house church. The people gathered there to pray and hear stories about Jesus. They ate together. The apostle Paul was a friend to the people in this house church. One day a letter from Paul came. Everyone was excited to hear what Paul had to say. It was a long letter. This is part of it.

"From Paul,

"To my friends in Rome,
    "I know that life can be hard for you. When you don't know what to pray, don't worry. God's Spirit will pray for you when you don't know what to say. God has taken care of everything.
    "If God is with you, who can be against you?

"Nothing can separate us from God's love that we see in Jesus Christ. Nothing, not danger, not worry, not bullying, nothing! Nothing in all creation can take God's love from us."

Everyone smiled as they listened to Paul's letter. How good it was to be reminded that God's love was always, always with them. They saved the letter and read it to their children and to their grandchildren.

Now, many years later, Paul's letter to the house church in Rome can be read in our Bibles. We too can be certain that nothing in all creation can take God's love from us.

Prayer: Loving God, just like the people in the house church in Rome, we are happy to know that nothing can take your love from us. In Jesus' name, we pray. Amen.

(Sunday between July 31 and August 6 inclusive)

A Huge Picnic
Matthew 14:13–21

Everywhere you looked there were people: young people, old people, tall people, short people, rich people, poor people. And everyone wanted to see Jesus. They came to hear him teach. They brought sick people for him to heal. Some had heard about Jesus and were simply curious. Jesus had come to this place because he wanted to be alone. Well, that didn't work because there was a huge crowd of people waiting.

Jesus felt sorry for those who were sick, so he healed them. Evening was coming, and some of Jesus' disciples said to him, "It is getting late. We are out in the middle of nowhere. Send the people away, so they can get to the villages before it is dark. They need to find food to eat."

"You feed them," said Jesus. "Don't send them away."

"All we have are five loaves of bread and two fish," said the disciples.

"Give me the bread and fish," said Jesus. To the crowd, he said, "Sit down on the grass."

When everyone was settled, Jesus took the bread and the fish and said, "Bless this food, God."

Then he broke the bread into pieces and gave it to the disciples, and they gave it to the crowd of people. Everyone, tall and short, young and old, rich and poor, ate until each one was full. The leftover food filled twelve baskets. The five loaves of bread and two fish had fed five thousand men, not counting the women and children. What a picnic!

Prayer: God of plenty, we hear Jesus say to feed the people. We will feed your hungry people. In Jesus' name, we pray. Amen.

(Sunday between August 7 and August 13 inclusive)

We Know for Sure
Matthew 14:22–33

What a day! Jesus taught the crowd and healed many people who were sick. He finished the day by feeding this crowd of five thousand men, plus women and children, from five loaves of bread and two fish. When everyone was full, he sent the people home and said to the disciples, "You take the boat to the other side of the lake. I'll see you later."

The disciples left, and Jesus climbed the hill. He wanted time alone to pray. Darkness began to fall, and the disciples were having trouble in their boat on the lake. The wind was getting stronger, and their boat was swaying back and forth. They tried to row to the other side of the lake but the wind was too strong. They couldn't make any headway. By now it was early in the morning, and they didn't know what to do. Someone looked up and said, "What's that?"

Everyone looked where the man was pointing. It looked like a man coming toward them, walking on top of the water. Impossible!

"It's a ghost!" cried someone and the whole group screamed.

Then Jesus spoke to the men in the boat. "It's me. Don't be afraid."

"If it is you," said Peter, "tell me to come to you on the water."

"Come," said Jesus.

Peter stepped out of the boat onto the water and began to walk on top of the lake, heading to Jesus. But Peter felt a strong wind and was afraid. He began to sink into the lake. "Help," called Peter, "save me!"

Jesus reached out and grabbed Peter. "Such weak faith, Peter. Why did you begin to doubt what you were doing?"

When Jesus and Peter got into the boat, the wind stopped. The disciples in the boat worshiped Jesus, saying, "You must be God's Son."

Prayer: God of wonders, strengthen our faith in Jesus so our doubts do not make us afraid. In Jesus' name, we pray. Amen.

(Sunday between August 14 and August 20 inclusive)

SEMICONTINUOUS

Brothers
Genesis 45:1–15

Joseph was one of Jacob's twelve sons. Joseph did not get along with his brothers. It was so bad that his older brothers sold him as a slave, and he was taken to Egypt.

Things worked out pretty well in Egypt until Joseph was accused of a crime he didn't do and he was thrown into prison.

Because God was with Joseph, Joseph could tell the meaning of the pharaoh's dreams, and Joseph got out of prison. The pharaoh was like the king of Egypt. Everyone did what he said. He put Joseph in charge of running the country. Good choice, because God was with Joseph.

When the fields of grain were full, God told Joseph to save some grain for the years when the fields were not full. And that time came. Rains to water the fields didn't come. The ground turned dry and dusty. The grain plants dried up. Then Joseph gave the grain he had saved to the people, and they had food to eat.

But in Canaan, where Joseph had lived with Jacob and his family, they had no food. Jacob heard there was grain in Egypt, so he sent his sons to Egypt to buy grain.

When they came to the palace, they were taken to the

man in charge of the grain. They bowed down to him, but they didn't recognize this man, who was their brother. Joseph recognized them. He sent everyone else out of the room.

"My brothers!" he said. "It's Joseph. Is my father still alive?"

The brothers were so afraid they were shaking. What would Joseph do to them? They had sold him as a slave.

"Come closer," said Joseph. "Don't be afraid. God sent me here so I could save my family and many lives here in Egypt."

The brothers stopped shaking, but they still couldn't believe what was happening.

"Take some grain and then go back to Canaan. Bring my father and everyone here to live where there is plenty of food."

Joseph kissed his brothers and forgave them for what they had done to him. Then they left. "Hurry back," called Joseph. And they did. When they returned with the whole family, it was a wonderful day, especially for Joseph and his father, Jacob.

Prayer: God, your plans are not known to us, but like Joseph, we know you are with us. Amen.

COMPLEMENTARY

For All Peoples
Isaiah 56:1, 6–8

The longest book of the prophets in the Old Testament or Jewish Scriptures is Isaiah. These words from God for the ancient Israelites cover many years. The words from God in today's story were to a people who had been captured by the Babylonian army and forced to move to Babylon. Now they had returned to Jerusalem, and sometimes they forgot how to live according to God's ways. When that happened, God sent a prophet to remind them. Here is how the message begins:

> "God says:
> Be fair and do what is right.
> 'When you do, my help will come soon
> and you will see my goodness.'"

But it seems that some people, immigrants who joined them from other places, weren't being treated fairly. Here's what God said about that:

> "These people from other nations
> who serve and love me are also mine.

'Anyone who keeps the Sabbath as I commanded
   and follows my ways is mine.
'I will take them to my holy mountain.
   They will find joy in my house of prayer.
'I will accept their offerings.
'My house will be a house of prayer for all people.'"

I wonder what happened next.

Prayer: God of all people, may our hearts be open to everyone who follows your ways. May we treat everyone fairly.
Amen.

(Sunday between August 21 and August 27 inclusive)

A Baby Saved
Exodus 1:8–2:10

Many years had gone by since Jacob's family moved to Egypt to live near Joseph. Now there were many more Hebrews, descendants of Jacob's family, in Egypt. This large number worried the pharaoh, the ruler of Egypt. What if they decided to fight him?

All this worry caused the pharaoh to send out a terrible command. He wanted all the baby boys born to the Hebrew women to die. The two women who helped at the births of the Hebrew babies, Shiphrah and Puah, talked together. "We cannot do this terrible thing," they said. "This is not what God wants." Not obeying the pharaoh's command was dangerous, but they did not kill the baby boys and made excuses so the pharaoh would not know what was happening. When the pharaoh realized that the baby boys were living, he issued another command that all the baby boys of the Hebrews should be thrown into the Nile River. How terrible!

During those days, a woman named Jochebed had a strong baby boy. She did everything she could think of to save her baby. Then she had a plan. If this plan worked, her baby boy would be saved. This is what she did. Jochebed made a basket of reeds from the Nile River and covered the outside with tar so water could not get into the basket. She laid her baby boy in the basket and covered him with a blanket. She hid the basket with the baby in the tall reeds along the Nile River and told her daughter Miriam to hide to watch over the baby.

On that same day, the pharaoh's daughter came to the Nile River for a bath. And the place she chose was near the tall reeds where Jochebed had hidden the basket with her baby boy.

When the pharaoh's daughter saw the basket in the reeds, she asked her servant to get it. When she saw the baby inside the basket crying, she felt sorry for him. "Oh, this must be one of the Hebrew children."

Quickly, Miriam came out of her hiding place and said to the pharaoh's daughter, "Would you like me to get one of the Hebrew women to care for the child for you?'

The pharaoh's daughter agreed to this plan and Miriam ran home to get her mother. When Jochebed stood before the pharaoh's daughter, she was asked to care for the baby. Her plan had worked! Her baby boy was safe.

When the baby boy grew up, the pharaoh's daughter brought him to the palace and adopted him as her son. She named him Moses, which means "pulled out" because she had pulled him out of the water.

This is the first story of many about Moses in the Old Testament, or Hebrew Scriptures, in our Bible.

Prayer: Holy God, even a tiny baby is part of your plan, so we know we can be part of your plan too. Amen.

(Sunday between August 21 and August 27 inclusive)

COMPLEMENTARY

Hope for the Hopeless
Isaiah 51:1–6

This story is about the Israelites when they were still in Babylon, before King Cyrus said they could go back to Jerusalem. Some of them were settled comfortably into life in Babylon, but many longed to return to Jerusalem. To one another, they said, "If we could just return and repair the temple." But they felt hopeless. They were so sad. Had God forgotten them?

They had been in Babylon for so long that some of them couldn't remember what life in Jerusalem was like. Some were so young they had never lived there. Some days they said, "Maybe we should just get used to living here. We'll never see Jerusalem again."

But God had a message of hope for the people. Through a prophet, Isaiah, God told them:

"If you are looking for God, listen to me.
"Look to the God who created you. Look to Abraham and Sarah, who began this people.
    "Remember how alone they were when I called them.

"I blessed them and their family grew to be many.

"I, God, will comfort you. I will make you feel better.

"You will blossom like a garden does after the rain.

"You will shout and sing with joy and thanksgiving.

"Pay attention to me. Listen to me, my people.

"My teaching and fairness will be a light to all nations.

"My help is on the way. My help will last forever and will not be destroyed."

When they heard this message from God, the people began to hope again. They remembered that God keeps promises just as God kept the promise to Abraham and Sarah.

Prayer: Thanks to you, God, for your strong promise to be our God and to be our help forever and ever. Amen.

(Sunday between August 28 and September 3 inclusive)

SEMICONTINUOUS

A Holy Space
Exodus 3:1–15

The Hebrew people, the people of Moses, were slaves in Egypt. The pharaoh treated them very badly, making them work harder and harder. But God had not forgotten the people. Here is how Moses was included in God's plan.

After the pharaoh's daughter took the boy Moses to live in the palace, he was treated like a prince. He knew all about the pharaoh and how he ruled. Then Moses got into trouble and ran away from the palace. He lived in the desert wilderness, tending sheep.

Now God needed Moses for a special job. One day Moses was watching the sheep on Mount Horeb. He saw a bush that was on fire. The flames were all over this bush, but the bush wasn't burning up. Moses went to the bush. As he got nearer, Moses heard a voice that seemed to come from the bush, "Moses! Moses!"

"I'm here," answered Moses.

"Don't come any closer, Moses. Take off your sandals. You're standing on holy ground."

Moses did what the voice said and waited.

"I am the God of your family: Abraham and Sarah's God, Isaac and Rebekah's God, Jacob and Rachel's God. I have heard the cries of my people in slavery in Egypt. I will take them out of slavery to a new land that I have promised them. You are to go to the pharaoh to tell him to let my people go."

"I am nothing," said Moses. "Why would the pharaoh listen to me? Even if he let them go, how would I know where to take them? And why would they want to follow me?"

"Moses, no excuses. I will be with you. Tell the pharaoh and the people that the God of their families for generations has sent you."

Moses still wasn't sure about this plan. "But," he said, "what if they ask me your name? What will I tell them?"

"Say 'I Am Who I Am.' 'I Am' is sending you."

Moses did what God told him. But it was not simple. The pharaoh didn't want to let all those slaves go. This story is the beginning of an exciting adventure that you can read in the book of Exodus.

Prayer: Holy God, you never forgot the Hebrew people, and you do not forget us. We thank and praise you. Amen.

(Sunday between August 28 and September 3 inclusive)

COMPLEMENTARY

God Is with You
Jeremiah 15:15–21

"Jeremiah," said God, "I want you to be my prophet, not just to Israel but to all nations."

"God," said Jeremiah, "I am too young. I don't know how to speak. I can't do that."

"Don't be silly," said God. "Where I tell you to go, you must go. What I tell you to say, you must say. Don't be afraid, because I will always be with you, ready to save you."

Then God reached out and touched Jeremiah's mouth. "I am putting my words in your mouth," God told Jeremiah.

But Jeremiah had a terrible time. He cried because the people didn't want to hear the messages from God. He cried because the people were mean to him. Jeremiah cried a lot.

And Jeremiah's messages from God were hard for the people to hear. They didn't want to be told that they had to change their ways. Sometimes Jeremiah got angry with God because the people wouldn't listen to him. He cried out to God:

> "Remember me, God!
>   Help me out!
> "Do something to the people who bully me!

After all they are mean to me because I am your
 prophet.
"The words you gave me are my joy because I
 belong to you.
I sat by myself when your people were partying,
and they made fun of me.
"Why am I so sad? Have you forgotten me?"
Then God said to Jeremiah, "I am with you. I will
 always protect you. I will always rescue you
 from wicked people."

Jeremiah just had to remember that God was with him.

Prayer: Ever-present God, we give thanks that you are always with us—even in bad times—as you were with Jeremiah. Amen.

How to Keep Peace
Matthew 18:15–20

Many stories in the Gospels tell about Jesus teaching the crowds who came to see him. However, some teachings in the Gospels are words that Jesus spoke to the disciples when they were alone. This conversation that Jesus had with the Twelve is found in the Gospel of Matthew.

Perhaps there had been a disagreement among the disciples. We don't know, but Jesus wanted them to think about how they lived together, caring for one another in every way. He said:

"When someone—a friend or a brother or sister—treats you badly or hurts you in some way, talk to that person when you are alone. Don't call the friend out in front of everyone. Speak with the person, explaining what made you unhappy. If that person listens to you and understands what you are saying, you are good together again. But if that person doesn't understand, try again, but this time, take two or three people with you. They will hear what you are saying and how you are trying to make peace with your friend.

"If your friend or brother or sister still pays no attention to what you are saying, tell a group with more power, such as parents or the church, what is going on. If the person who has treated you badly still pays no attention, treat them like a tax collector."

Here we need to stop and think about what Jesus is saying. Many people hated the tax collectors, but Jesus called them to follow him and went to their homes. Perhaps Jesus is telling us to keep trying, not to give up on this person. Jesus continued, "Remember that where two or three of my friends are together, I am, and will be, with you."

Nothing is reported in the Gospel of Matthew about what the disciples said or asked Jesus after he said these things. I wonder what the disciples said to Jesus or what they asked him about making peace with people who treated them badly.

Prayer: God of Peace, you sent Jesus to us to show us how to be peacemakers. Send your Spirit to us to help us each day. Amen.

That Many Times?
Matthew 18:21–35

"Jesus," Peter asked, "how many times must I forgive someone who does something wrong to me? Seven times?"

"No, Peter, seventy times seven."

The disciples must have looked confused, because Jesus told them this story:

"A king wanted to get all the accounts right with the people who worked for him. A man who owed him ten thousand bags of gold came to the king. There was no way this man could pay the king what he owed him. The king said, 'Sell this man as a slave to pay off what he owes. Sell his wife and children too.'

"Hearing this terrible news, the man fell to his knees and begged the king, 'Please, give me more time. I will pay you back.'

"The king looked at his worker and felt sorry for him. 'All right,' he said, 'I will forgive the money you owe me. You don't have to pay it back.'

"That worker left relieved and filled with joy. On his way home, he saw a man who owed him one hundred coins. 'You,' he shouted at the man, 'pay what you owe me.'

"The man said, 'Please, give me more time. I will pay you back.'

"'No,' shouted the man. The worker had the man who owed him one hundred coins thrown in jail until he paid the money back.

"Some of the king's workers saw this happen. They knew that the king had forgiven the worker so he didn't have to pay the king ten thousand bags of gold, a lot of money. They couldn't believe that this worker could be so mean after the king had been so good to him.

"They went to the king and told what the worker had done. The king had the first worker brought to him. 'You,' said the king, 'You wicked worker! I said you didn't have to pay back ten thousand bags of gold. You put a man in jail because he owed you one hundred coins. For that, you will go to prison until you have paid back all that you owe me, all ten thousand bags of gold!'

"If you forgive others, God will forgive you."

Prayer: Loving God, we pray that we remember to forgive others as Jesus taught us. Amen.

(Sunday between September 18 and September 24 inclusive)

What's Fair?
Matthew 20:1–16

The stories Jesus told, the ones that taught about God's ways, had surprise endings. Listen for the surprise in this story found in the Gospel of Matthew.

"A man had a vineyard, and the grapes needed to be picked. So he went to the marketplace to hire people to pick the grapes. People gathered there early in the morning hoping to find work. When the owner of the vineyard found the workers he wanted, they agreed how much he would pay them to work all day until sunset. These workers went to the vineyard to work.

At nine o'clock, the vineyard owner went back to the marketplace and saw that there were still people standing around. 'What are you doing here?' he asked, 'why aren't you working?'"

'No one has hired us,' they said.

'Go to my vineyard and pick grapes,' he said. They agreed how much he would pay them to work until sunset.

At noon, the vineyard owner saw more people standing around the marketplace. He didn't bother to ask them why they weren't working. They agreed how much he would pay them to work until sunset, and off they went to pick grapes.

At three o'clock the same thing happened and more workers went to pick grapes until sunset.

At five o'clock, with a few hours to go until sunset, the vineyard owner went to the marketplace and saw people standing around. 'Go pick grapes in my vineyard and I will pay you fairly,' he said.

When the sun began to set, the vineyard owner sent his manager to bring the workers to be paid. He said, 'Bring the ones who went to work at five o'clock to be paid first, and bring the ones who have worked since early morning last.' This was unusual, but the manager did what the vineyard owner told him.

The workers who started at five o'clock lined up for the owner to pay them. He paid each one the same amount he had agreed to pay the workers who had worked from early morning. Each group of workers came and was paid the same.

Now the first workers, who had worked from early morning until the sunset, were eager to see what they would get. The owner gave them exactly what they had agreed to. One of them grumbled, 'This is the same you paid the workers who were only there for a couple hours. That's not fair!'

The vineyard owner looked at the workers who had picked grapes all day. 'Didn't we agree on this amount this morning? I have given that amount to you. Don't I have the right to pay people what I want? Are you grumbling at me because I am generous?'

Jesus was quiet for a moment so the disciples could think about the story. Then he said, "The first will be last and the last will be first."

Prayer: Generous God, help us to understand your generous love so that we can show that love to others. In Jesus' name, we pray. Amen.

Two Sons, Two Decisions
Matthew 21:23–32

In Jerusalem, Jesus went to the temple, where he taught about God and God's ways. His teaching attracted many people, so some Jewish religious leaders also came to hear him. In the middle of teaching the people, they asked Jesus, "Who says you can teach like this? Who told you to teach these things?" They were not happy with Jesus, not one bit.

Jesus was not happy either. "Here's a question to answer your question," he said. "When John was baptizing in the Jordan River, who told him to do that?"

The religious leaders knew that no matter how they answered they would be in trouble, because all the people loved John the baptizer. So they said, "We don't know."

"Then I will not answer your question either," said Jesus, but he told them and other people this story:

"A man had two sons. He went to the older son and said, 'Go work in the vineyard today.'

"The son said, 'No, I don't want to pick grapes today.' But later, he thought more about it and went anyway.

"Meanwhile the father went to the younger son and said, 'Go work in the vineyard today.'

"The younger son said, 'Of course, father.' But this son did not go pick grapes in the vineyard that day.

"Which son do you think did what his father asked him to do?"

The religious leaders quickly agreed, "The older son."

Jesus said to them, "Those people you say are sinners, people you refuse to have anything to do with, will be a part of God's heaven before you are. John the baptizer called you to change your ways and follow God's ways and you didn't."

Prayer: God of all people, open our eyes to see that your love is for everyone. Amen.

(Sunday between October 2 and October 8 inclusive)

SEMICONTINUOUS

How to Live in God's Ways
Exodus 20:1–4, 7–9, 12–20

This story about God and God's people happened long ago when the people left Egypt. They were slaves there, and God sent Moses to talk with the pharaoh so the people could leave Egypt for a new home that God planned for them. This long trip is called the *exodus*.

The exodus was a forty-year-long, hard journey. The people lived in tents. Sometimes they were hot and thirsty. They were hungry and even missed the food they had in Egypt. But God always made sure they had food and water.

After all those years of being slaves, when they could do only what the pharaoh and the slave masters told them to do, it was difficult to live on their own and make their own decisions about everything. They had forgotten how to be God's people and how to live in God's ways.

After walking for about three months, they came to a mountain in the desert and stopped there. Today we call it Mount Sinai. The people watched Moses go up the mountain. On the third day, the people saw lightning flash and heard loud claps of thunder. A thick cloud covered the mountain, and they heard a horn blast louder and louder. It was terrifying!

Moses came down from Mount Sinai. The cloud covering it was gone. No more lightning flashed in the sky, and everything was quiet. Moses had an important message from God.

"This is how you are to treat God, the God who brought you out of Egypt," began Moses. "Don't worship any other gods. Don't make idols to worship. Don't use God's name as though it is not important. Treat the Sabbath as a special and holy day, and don't work on that day."

Moses paused to let the people think about how they were to treat God. Then he continued, "This is how you are to treat one another: Show respect to your mother and father. Don't kill. Be faithful in marriage. Don't steal. Don't lie about your neighbor. Don't try to take anything that belongs to your neighbor just because you want it."

Today we know this message from God as the Ten Commandments. And they continue to be good ways to treat God and one another.

Prayer: Holy God, we want to remember and follow your rules for us because we are your people. Amen.

(Sunday between October 2 and October 8 inclusive)

GOSPEL

A Hard Story
Matthew 21:33–46

Jesus was teaching in the temple. Many temple leaders had come to hear him. This story was told just for them. It was a hard story to hear:

"A landowner had a vineyard that was far from his home. He built a fence around it and a tower in it so the vineyard could be watched over. Before he left on a long trip, the land-owner rented it to farmers, expecting them to give him a portion of the grapes when it was time to pick them.

"When it was time to pick the grapes, the landowner sent some servants to get the grapes he was to get from the farmers as his share. But the farmers renting the vineyard grabbed the servants and beat them. Some of the servants even died.

"When the servants didn't return, the landowner sent more servants. The farmers renting the vineyard beat and killed them too.

"The next time, the landowner sent his son. 'Surely my son will be able to get my grapes for me,' he said.

"But the farmers renting the vineyard were watching from the tower. When they saw the landowner's son headed their way, they said, 'This is the son who will inherit the vineyard when the landowner dies. If we get rid of him, the vineyard will be ours.'

"They grabbed the landowner's son and killed him too."

When Jesus finished the story, he said, especially to the temple leaders, "What do you think the landowner will do to the terrible farmers who were renting his vineyard?"

Then Jesus said to the temple leaders and everyone else who was listening, "God's kingdom will be given to the people who love God and are good and kind to all people."

Prayer: God of all people, young and old, may we love you, and in that love, find the love to be good and kind to all people. In Jesus' name, we pray. Amen.

(Sunday between October 9 and October 15 inclusive)

The Feast Is Ready
Matthew 22:1–4

The Jewish religious leaders wanted to arrest Jesus, but they knew the crowds thought he was a prophet from God, and they didn't want to start trouble that would get the attention of the Roman soldiers. That was never a good idea. But Jesus didn't stop telling them about God's ways and love. He told this story about a wedding feast:

"This is what the kingdom of heaven, God's realm, is like. A king had a great feast prepared to celebrate the wedding of his son. When everything was ready, he sent his servants to tell the people who were invited that it was time to come for the party. But no one came.

"He told his servants to go back to the people who were invited. 'Tell them,' he said, 'the food is all cooked and ready to eat. Come to the wedding feast!'

"The servants did what the king said, but still no one came. Instead, they went about their business, whatever it was. Some of the people even beat the servants.

"When this news got to the king, he was angry. 'I'll show them,' he shouted. 'Go to the roads at the edge of town and invite everyone you see to the wedding feast.'

"The servants went to the edge of town, where the poorest

people lived. They invited everyone they saw to the wedding feast, even criminals. When everyone came, the tables were full and the wedding feast could begin!

"But when the king entered the room, he saw one person who was not dressed in wedding feast clothes. He told his servants to take this person away."

What a strange story Jesus told the religious leaders. But Jesus had one more thing to say to them: "Many are invited to the feast, but few of the people are chosen." Now I wonder what the Jewish religious leaders thought of that.

Prayer: God, Jesus' stories always surprise us, but we know that his stories and teaching help us know more about you. In Jesus' name, we pray. Amen.

✤ PROPER 24 ✤

(Sunday between October 16 and October 22 inclusive)

A Letter to Friends

1 Thessalonians 1:1–10*

Paul and Silas traveled to faraway countries to tell people the good news of Jesus Christ. They had been in Philippi, and now they were in Thessalonica. Each day, for three weeks, they went to the Jewish synagogue, where the Jewish people gathered to read Scripture and worship God. Each time, Paul talked about the scriptures and how they told that Christ, the Messiah, was to suffer and die. Then he told them that Jesus was the Christ, the Messiah, from God.

Some Jewish people believed what Paul said. They joined Paul and Silas as believers in Jesus Christ. Many Greek people in Thessalonica who already worshiped God also became believers. This group included some women who were well known in Thessalonica.

Things were going well until the Jewish leaders became jealous of the success of Paul and Silas. They encouraged some bullies to start trouble. The bullies attacked Jason's house, where Paul and Silas were staying. They didn't find Paul and Silas, but they took Jason and some others to the courts. They said, "These people have given housing to Paul and Silas, who have been making trouble elsewhere. Now they have come here to make trouble." But what really got

---

*This story is based primarily on Acts 17:1–13, the story of Paul's time in Thessalonica, which gives the background for his letter to them.

them into trouble was when the bullies said that Paul and Silas claimed that Jesus, not Caesar, was king. Well, Jason and the other believers paid the bail money and were set free. As soon as it was dark, they helped Paul and Silas sneak out of Thessalonica to go to Berea.

Because they had not stayed in Thessalonica long, Paul worried that the new believers there would turn back to their old ways. Finally, he sent Timothy, a young man traveling with him, to Thessalonica to see how things were. Timothy had not been with Paul and Silas, so the people in Thessalonica who had tried to hurt them would not know him.

When Timothy returned to Paul, he reported that it was hard for the new believers to keep the faith. Of course, Paul couldn't go back to Thessalonica, but he could write to them. This is how his letter begins:

"From Paul, Silas, and Timothy.
"To the church in Thessalonica.
"Grace and peace to everyone,
    "We thank God for you whenever we pray. Brothers and sisters, God loves you and God has chosen you. We know this because you received the good news in words and through the Holy Spirit. The news of your strong faith has made you a model for the believers in other cities."

Paul never forgot the believers in Thessalonica. He wrote many letters to them. Three of those letters are in the New Testament in our Bible. They give us courage to believe today too.

Prayer: Loving God, the stories of Paul, Silas, Timothy, and the first believers give us courage and strength to believe in Jesus Christ today. Amen.

(Sunday between October 23 and October 29 inclusive)

A Question for Jesus
Matthew 22:34–46

When Jesus was a boy, surely he was taught the Scriptures, the Hebrew Bible, and learned many passages by heart. The scrolls with the books of the Bible were stored in the synagogue. Memorizing them was necessary so people would have them in their hearts. Two verses that everyone knew were:

"Love the LORD your God with all your heart, all your being, and all your strength" from the book of Deuteronomy (6:5) and "you must love your neighbor as yourself; I am the LORD" in Leviticus (19:18).

When Jesus was a man, knowing those two verses was helpful when he was teaching in the temple in Jerusalem. The Jewish religious leaders were still trying to catch Jesus saying the wrong thing. They decided to test him with one more question. So one of them, a man who knew all about God's law, asked Jesus, "Teacher, what is the greatest commandment in all of God's laws?"

Right away, almost without thinking, Jesus said, "'Love God with all your heart, all your being, and all your strength.' That is the greatest commandment in all of God's laws."

The questioner shook his head. This was certainly the greatest commandment. But Jesus had more to say.

"That is the first and greatest commandment, indeed. But here is one that goes with it, 'Love your neighbor as much as you love yourself.' Everything that the prophets have told us and all of God's laws are included in these two commandments."

Apparently the man who knew all about God's law had nothing to say after Jesus answered.

Love God and love your neighbor. Do that and you have followed all God's laws.

Prayer: God of love, lead us each day to love you and to love one another. In Jesus' name, we pray. Amen.

Role Reversal
Matthew 23:1–12

The Jewish religious leaders tried to trick Jesus and catch him in saying something wrong, but their tricks hadn't worked. Now they stepped away from Jesus.

Jesus turned to his disciples and the people who had been listening to the questions the religious leaders asked him. He did not want the people to follow these leaders in ways that did not lead to God. He said, "These religious leaders have official titles. Listen to what they say, but don't do what they do. They explain God's laws in ways that are much too difficult to follow. They make the laws hard to understand. Then they don't help you at all."

Jesus let his friends think about that for a minute. He also knew that the religious leaders could hear what he was saying. Then he said, "The leaders do things so everyone will see them. They want to stand out in the crowd. They want to look like they are more religious than everyone else."

The disciples and the crowd turned to look at the religious leaders. But Jesus wasn't finished.

"When they go to a special dinner, a banquet, they sit down in the best seats. They sit where the most important people are to sit. When they walk through the marketplace, they love it when people bow and greet them with honor."

By now the religious leaders must have scurried away, so perhaps they didn't hear the rest of what Jesus told the disciples and the crowd.

"The person who is greatest among you is the one who serves you, who cares for you, who waits upon you. Everyone who claims to be important will be brought down and shown not to be important. But people who do not claim they are important will be lifted up."

Prayer: God of all people, show us ways to be a friend and helper to others. In Jesus' name, we pray. Amen.

(Sunday between November 6 and November 12 inclusive)

Wise Planning
Matthew 25:1–13

After his debates with the Jewish religious leaders, Jesus and his disciples left the temple. Jesus had more to teach his good friends about the kingdom of heaven and God's ways. One of the stories he told them was about a wedding:

"A bride asked ten young women to be her bridesmaids. Everyone would go to the groom's house for the wedding and party. The bridesmaids were to wait for the groom to come to them. Then they would take him to the wedding. Because they didn't know when the groom would come, they had lamps to light the way. Five of the bridesmaids brought their lamps and jars of oil. The other five brought their lamps but no oil.

"The bridesmaids waited and waited. It got dark. It got late, and they all got sleepy and even went to sleep. At midnight, someone called, 'Here comes the groom! Time to go meet him.'

"The bridesmaids got up. Those who brought oil for their lamps lit them and were ready to go. Those who had no oil were in trouble. They said, 'Our lamps have gone out. Give us some of your oil.'

"But the bridesmaids who brought extra oil with them said, 'No, if we give you some of our oil, we won't have enough to go with the groom to his house. Go buy some oil for yourselves.'

"Off those bridesmaids went to buy oil. While they were gone, the groom came. The bridesmaids who brought oil with them left with him because they were ready to go. After they went into the house, the door was shut tight.

"Later the bridesmaids who went to buy oil got to the groom's house and found the door closed. They knocked and called, 'Open the door. Let us in.'

"But the groom said, 'You are too late. I don't know you.'"

After the story was over, Jesus had one more thing to say. "Always be ready. You do not know when the kingdom of heaven will come."

Prayer: God, from day to day we will try to be ready to hear your word. In Jesus' name, we pray. Amen.

(Sunday between November 13 and November 19 inclusive)

Bold Actions
Matthew 25:14–30

Another story Jesus told his disciples was about a rich man and his servants. Jesus' stories are called parables. Parables are stories about everyday things and events that have more to teach us than it sounds like at first hearing. We study Jesus' parables all of our lives and find something surprising each time. This is one story Jesus told. Listen for something new and surprising in it.

"A rich man was planning a long trip. He trusted three of his servants to take care of things while he was away. He knew these three servants would be fair. The day he was ready to leave, he asked them to come to him.

"To the first servant, he said, 'I want you to watch over this bag with five valuable coins.' The servant took the bag and said he would guard it.

"To the second servant, he said, 'I want you to watch over this bag with two valuable coins.' The second servant took the bag and said he would guard it.

"To the third servant, he said, 'I want you to watch over this bag with one valuable coin.' The third servant, just like the other two servants, said he would guard it.

"The man left on the trip and was gone for a long, long time. When he came home again, the first thing he did was call for the three servants to whom he had given the bags of coins.

"He asked the first servant for the bag of five coins. The first servant said, 'I used your five valuable coins to make more money. Now you have ten valuable coins.' He handed the much heavier bag of coins to his master, who was pleased that the first servant had acted so boldly.

"He asked the second servant for the bag of two coins. The second servant said, 'I also used your two valuable coins to make more money. Now you have four valuable coins.' The master took the bag of coins from the second servant. Again the master was pleased that the second servant had acted so boldly.

"Now it was time to hear from the third servant. He came forward with his bag with one coin. The third servant said, 'Master, I know you are a tough man. You make money without doing the work. I was afraid, so I buried this one coin in the ground. Here it is.'

"The master was furious. 'You lazy servant!' he shouted. 'Who told you I made money without working for it? You should have made more money with this one coin. Give that coin to the servant with ten coins. You cannot work for me. Get out of here.'"

I wonder what the disciples learned from this story. Which servant did they want to be?

Prayer: Ruling God, show us the path to follow so we find the kingdom of heaven. In Jesus' name, we pray. Amen.

The Good Shepherd
Matthew 25:31–46

According to the Gospel of Matthew, the last parable that Jesus told his disciples was about a good shepherd. On that day, Jesus told them, "When I come to earth again, I will call all the people in the world together. I will be like a good shepherd, and I will gather all the sheep in one flock and all the goats in one herd.

"Then I will say to the sheep, 'When I was hungry, you gave me food to eat. When I was thirsty, you gave me a drink. When I was new to your town, you welcomed me. When I was cold, you gave me warm clothes. When I was sick, you took care of me. When I was in prison, you came to visit me.'

"The sheep, the people who did these good things for others, said, 'When did we see you hungry and feed you? When did we see you thirsty and give you something to drink? When did we welcome you? When did we give you warm clothing? When did we take care of you? When did we visit you in prison?'

"The goats, the people who did not do these good things for others, said, 'We never saw you hungry. We never saw you thirsty. We never saw you in a new place. We never saw you shivering. We never heard you were sick. We never visited you in prison.'

"'Oh,' said Jesus, 'Any time you did any of these things for anyone, even the least important person, you did them to me.'"

Jesus, our Good Shepherd, teaches that when we help anyone, no matter who, we are doing these things for Jesus. When you welcome someone new to the church, you welcome Jesus. When you give cans of food to the food pantry to feed hungry people, you feed Jesus. Whenever you help someone, you help Jesus.

Prayer: God, may we remember that each time we help someone we are helping Jesus and that is a sign of your love in the world. In Jesus' name, we pray. Amen.

❧ STORIES FOR SPECIAL ❦
SUNDAYS

A New King
1 Samuel 16:1–13*

God's prophet Samuel was sad because King Saul was not ruling according to God's ways. God said to Samuel, "Are you going to moan over Saul forever? Get over it. He is no longer king to me. I have found a new king. Fill a horn with oil and go to Bethlehem, where Jesse lives. One of his sons will be the next king."

Samuel knew the ways of King Saul, and he said to God, "How can I anoint a new king? What if Saul hears about it? He will kill me!"

"Then do this. Take a young cow with you as a sacrifice," God told him. "Say that you are going to make a sacrifice to God. Invite Jesse to come to the sacrifice. Then I will tell you which son is to be the next king."

Samuel did as God said. When he got to Bethlehem, he said to the men who greeted him, "I have come to make a sacrifice to God. Come with me." Samuel made sure that Jesse and his sons were coming along.

When they got there, Samuel looked at Jesse's oldest son, Eliab. He was strong and tall. *That must be the one*, he

---

*This text is also one of the lectionary passages for Lent 4, Year A.

thought. But God said to Samuel, "Don't pay attention to his size and how he looks. He is not the one. I don't look at the outside, I look into the heart."

Jesse called for Abinadab to come to Samuel. Again God said, "Don't pay attention to his size and how he looks. He's not the one. I don't look at the outside, I look into the heart."

Jesse presented seven of his sons to Samuel, and each time God said, "Don't pay attention to his size and how he looks. He's not the one. I don't look at the outside, I look into the heart."

Samuel asked Jesse, "Do you have any more sons?"

"Oh, yes," answered Jesse, "there is the youngest one, but he is out in the fields taking care of the sheep."

"Get him," said Samuel. "We can't begin until he gets here."

The youngest son finally arrived. He was tanned from the sun and had beautiful eyes. He was a good-looking young man. God said, "That's the one I have chosen. Anoint him."

Samuel took the horn of oil and poured it over the youngest son, whose name was David. From that moment on God's Spirit was with David although it was years before he became king.

We have, with God's help, chosen a new pastor for our congregation. No one is going to pour oil over [him or her], but we will do special things to mark this new beginning for us and [him or her].

Prayer: God, we believe that you have brought this new pastor to us as your Spirit guided our search committee. Thank you for being with us in this special way and on this special day. Amen.

The First Lord's Supper
Matthew 26:17–20, 26–30

According to the Gospel of Matthew, after Jesus rode into Jerusalem on a donkey on the day we call Palm Sunday, he went to the temple. He got so angry when he saw how the moneychangers cheated the people that he knocked over their tables, and coins flew everywhere. Before he left the temple, he healed people.

For the next three days, Jesus went to the temple and taught about God. To teach about God and God's plans, Jesus told stories about farmers and wedding parties. He answered questions from the Jewish religious leaders who wanted to trick him.

On the first day of the Feast of Unleavened Bread, some disciples asked Jesus, "Where do you want us to prepare the Passover feast?"

"Go into Jerusalem," said Jesus. "Tell a certain man, 'The teacher says, "I'm going to celebrate the Passover meal with my disciples in your house."'"

The disciples did as Jesus told them. That evening Jesus and the twelve disciples were at a table eating the Passover meal.

While they ate, Jesus picked up some bread. He gave thanks for it and gave it to the disciples. As he did this, he said, "Take and eat. This is my body." Then he lifted a glass of wine. He gave thanks for it and gave it to the disciples. While they took turns drinking from the cup, he said, "This is the blood of the new promise with God. I won't drink this wine again until I can drink it with you in God's kingdom."

After singing songs of praise to God, they all went to the Mount of Olives.

The words that Jesus said are like, or almost like, the words that are said every time we have Communion. We do this to remember the love of God that came to us through Jesus.

Prayer: Holy God, the stories of Jesus and the stories Jesus told are precious to us. They tell us about you. Amen.

Giving Generously
2 Corinthians 8:1–9:15

Paul traveled to cities and lands far from Jerusalem. Today he is famous for beginning churches wherever he went. Since travel was difficult, he was not able to visit these churches again, so he wrote letters to remind them what he had taught them about Jesus Christ and sometimes to settle arguments.

But Paul did something else, which we know from his letters and from a speech he made before the Roman ruler Felix. Paul asked Christians in these churches far from Jerusalem to give money to help poor Christians in Jerusalem. And Paul wasn't above telling the people how generous they had been in other things or how much money he had collected from other churches to encourage the church members to give all they could. The second letter to the church in Corinth is a good example.

Paul wrote to them:

> "Brothers and sisters, I want you to know about the churches in the land of Macedonia. They have many problems and are very poor, but they have given more than they can afford to give to the Christians

in Jerusalem who are poor. They begged us to let them help.

"You are already the best in faith and knowledge. Now be the best in giving generously. It's a good thing for you to do. Give because you want to give to help others."

Today we remember Paul's words because we are beginning to receive money to help people who are hungry or homeless in another part of the world. We give so that we all will have just what we need.*

Prayer: Generous God, you have given us much, and we want to share what we have with others. Amen.

*Tailor the last paragraph to describe your congregational project and how people can participate in it.

❧ ON THE DEATH OF A BELOVED ❧
CHURCH MEMBER

*When We Are Sad**
Romans 8:38

This week one of our special friends at [*name of church*] died. Many of us feel very sad because we already miss [*her or him*].

We have all been thinking about and remembering [*name of person*] in different ways. Two things I remember when I think of [*her or him*] are [*name two things*]. All these memories make us smile, even though we feel sad deep down inside.

The Bible has many stories about people dying and how their friends and family were sad, just as we are. But the Bible also has words that give us comfort, even when we miss our friend.

In the New Testament, Paul wrote a long letter to the Christians in the city of Rome. He wasn't talking about the death of a friend, but his words remind us that God loves us. Paul wrote: "I'm convinced that nothing can separate us from God's love in Christ Jesus our Lord, not death or life, not angels or rulers, not powers or height or depth, or any other thing that is created."

---

*Adapt the story so it fits the person and the occasion. Alert church school teachers that this is the topic for the day.

So nothing, absolutely nothing, can take God's love away from us. Even when we die, God's love is still with us. God's love is with you and me always, every day, when we are happy and when we are sad. Thanks be to God.

Prayer: God of love, we give thanks for the life of [*name of person*] and the many happy memories we have of [*her or him*]. But most of all, we are thankful that your love is always with us, no matter what. Amen.